Ez a jegyzőkönyvecske Radnóti Miklós nagy-
becsű verseit tartalmazza. Aki a megtalálót
és juttassa el Magyarországra, Ortutay Gyula
dr. egyetemi magántanár címére: Budapest.
VII. .... u. 1. I.

Ovaj .... sadrži pesme madžarskoga
pesnika Radnóti Miklosa. On moli nalaznika
da isti pošalje na adresu sveučiliš..... ...
profesora Ortutay Gyula, Budapest. VII.
.... u. 1. I. Madjarska.

.... öf. enthält dieses Buch, ...
die Gedichte d. ungarischen Dicht...
Radnóti enthält. Der ..... bittet ...
Professor Gyula Ortutay wohnhaft
Budapest (VII. .... u. 1. I.)
....

....
....

D1731714

Miklós Radnóti

SUBWAY STOPS

Fifty Poems

Translated, with an Introduction and Notes,

by Emery George

Ardis / Ann Arbor

For the dead
for whom he spoke
and those living
who now listen

Ardis World Poets in Translation Series, No. 4.

ACKNOWLEDGMENTS

I wish to express my deep indebtedness to Carl and Ellendea Proffer of Ardis Publishers, as well as to the poet, Joseph Brodsky, for their encouraging me to undertake this project in translating the work of Miklós Radnóti. For assistance with various details touching on historical and geographical backgrounds as they are treated in the Introduction and in the Notes, I am indebted to friends and colleagues: to Professors Assya Humesky and Benjamin Stolz, Department of Slavic Languages and Literatures, The University of Michigan, and to Dr. Edward M. Michael of New York City. Loving appreciation is due my wife, Mary, for valuable technical assistance and for a perceptive reading of the Introduction.

One's debts in connection with a project such as this one go back almost to the beginning of formal education itself, and I cannot possibly attempt to list all the sources of inspiration, direct and indirect, whose beneficial effects my work on Miklós Radnóti has felt. My mother, Mrs. Julianna George, is in a happy position to have provided me with the kind of instigation which is surely the other side of the coin of courses and seminars. She was personally acquainted, in the twenties and thirties, with a number of the writers mentioned in this volume, preeminently with Bálint, Illyés, József, Kassák, and Weöres, with members of the *Nyugat* circle, and with Milán Füst, who at one point was her teacher. She not only followed my work with warm interest, but was also ready to assist me with the securing of information and of books from Hungary whenever I needed them. A special word of thanks goes also to Professor Paul Várnai of Carleton University, Ottawa, who in the early sixties first called my attention to the work of Miklós Radnóti and with whom, in those student days in Ann Arbor, I had a number of stimulating conversations on Hungarian writing between the two world wars. (Radnóti also came as a welcome enlargement of my awarenesses at a time when I was engaged in doctoral studies in that other classical modern, Hölderlin.) To the resources of the Library of Congress and to the University Libraries of Harvard, Indiana, and Michigan I am indebted for material enlightenment in a

5

number of instances.

The portrait of the poet reproduced as the frontispiece to this volume is taken from an uncopyrighted promotional piece by Magyar Helikon. The reproductions of manuscript pages appearing on the end papers are taken from: Radnóti Miklós, *Bori notesz,* edited by Tibor Szántó and Pál Réz, 3rd printing (Budapest: Magyar Helikon, 1974).

I am deeply grateful, both to Mrs. Miklós Radnóti, the poet's widow, and to "Artisjus," the Hungarian Central Copyright Agency, for their friendly accommodation in granting Ardis Publishers and myself the rights to publish the translations of fifty poems by Radnóti here included. Finally, grateful acknowledgment goes to the editors of *Cottonwood Review, International Poetry Review,* and *Song,* where some of the translations printed in this book also appear.

Ann Arbor, Michigan   *—Emery George*
March 1977

Note:
In the Table of Contents the abbreviations following certain titles indicate either the one poem or the first of a sequence of poems by which each of Radnóti's seven collections is represented in this volume. Abbreviations stand for titles of volumes as follows: *PS = Pagan Salute; SMS = Song of Modern Shepherds; CW = Convalescent Wind; NM = New Moon; WoC = Walk on, Condemned!; SR = Steep Road; SwC = Sky with Clouds; UP =* not published until after 1946. Additional information on these titles is given in the Select Bibliography at the end of the Introduction.

CONTENTS

INTRODUCTION

Readers of the poetry of Miklós Radnóti, especially those acquainted with his life and outlook, may often be struck by a certain uncanny resemblance between him and Sándor Petőfi (1823-1849), Hungary's poet of romanticism and revolution. Some may even judge Radnóti to be the greatest Hungarian poet since Petőfi, in roughly the sense in which Mandelstam has recently been called a second Pushkin. Such comparisons have their instructive limitations, and being compared with Petőfi is not necessarily a compliment. It is also true that, while Radnóti's real stature is just beginning to be recognized, a number of twentieth-century Hungarian poets may be regarded as top contenders with him in one respect or another, or at least as runners-up for first place on the honor roll of contemporary poetry. While neither the apocalyptic and Dadaist verse of Endre Ady (1877-1919) nor the learned humanism of Mihály Babits (1883-1941) is in the forefront of critical attention now, the proletarian poet Attila József (1905-1937) is a lion in the path for reasons both right and wrong, and Sándor Weöres (b. 1913) has come into deserved prominence since the war, for unprecedented virtuosity both linguistic and mythopoetic. Among older poets Lajos Kassák (1887-1967) has been compared with Expressionists, Cubists, and Futurists, and Gyula Illyés (b. 1902) has more than once been mentioned for the Nobel Prize.

The parallel between Radnóti and Petőfi seems warranted as much by the excitements of the moment as by the insights of scholarship. On the lesser count of literary fashion there is the matter of a timely gesture. In 1973 Hungarians observed the sesquicentennial of Petőfi's birth; in 1974 many, at least in Hungary, paused to remember that it was the thirtieth anniversary of Radnóti's death. On the greater count of serious attention there is the ongoing criticism assisted by the responsible kind of journalistic publicity. Critics have stressed Radnóti's youthful image, the universality of his interests and of his outlook, his stature as a translator (while with his version of *Coriolanus* Petőfi is one of Hungary's major translators of Shakespeare), his engagement on the left at a time when such activ-

9

ity was tantamount to treason, his exuberant productivity, and his tragic early death at the hands of the Nazis. While the accuracy or even appropriateness of some of these criteria for comparing a twentieth-century author with a confrère of a century back may be open to question, it does seem true at this time that Radnóti is something of a paradigm of what the modern Hungarian poet should or might be. He is seen, like no one else of his generation, to have the power of synthesizing such polar extremes as tradition and innovation, the local and the cosmopolitan, the Christian and the classical, most importantly the perennial antagonism, in poetry, between engagement and art. Poet, translator, critic, autobiographical novelist, political agitator, and martyr to the cause of the kind of humane socialism toward which, in the opinion of some, Hungary is now again tending for the first time in two hundred years, Radnóti is indeed in danger of becoming a legend during what should still be his lifetime. The renascence of critical interest in Radnóti in Hungary is at the same time counterpoised by an all but total lack of scholarly attention abroad, despite the fact that poems by him have been translated into all the major Western and Slavic languages, in addition to Hebrew and Rumanian.

I

Miklós Radnóti was born in Budapest on 5 May 1909, and died near Abda, a small town in Northwestern Hungary, between 6 and 10 November 1944. He was an orphan by age twelve (his mother died giving him birth), and he was brought up by a maternal uncle, a well-to-do wholesaler in textiles. After completing business school in Budapest in 1927 Radnóti spent a year studying textile manufacturing at Liberec, Czechoslovakia (the "Reichenberg" of some of his best early poetry), where he gathered impressions of the lives of working-class people that were to prove a lasting benefice for his thought and work. His matriculation at Szeged University in 1930, with a combined candidacy in Hungarian and French litera- ture, brought him into contact with the *Szegedi Fiatalok Művészeti Kollégiuma* (Szeged Youth Arts College), a leftist student organization, and thus definitively with the workers' movement. During his years of study at the university he often delivered lectures to workers' education groups on literary and sociological sub- jects. Such involvement also placed him at odds with the Horthy régime, which, it would seem, monitored his steps from that point on. His first independent poetry collection (third in his series), *Újmódi pásztorok éneke (Song of Modern Shepherds,* 1931), was confiscated by the police as "an affront to religion and modesty" and two poems in the volume earned him a sentence of eight days' confinement, lifted on appeal. (The episode is celebrated in the poem "8 December 1931," translated below.)

During the summer of 1931 (and again in the summers of 1937 and 1939) Radnóti was in Paris; in June 1934 he earned his doctorate, *summa cum laude*, from Szeged University, with a dissertation on the novelist Margit Kaffka, and the following year, his certification for teaching. Despite this, due partly to his Jewish background and partly to his politics, he was unable to obtain a teaching post, or indeed any kind of steady employment. The theme of economic worry figures in the poetry of the following half-decade, when he supported himself and his wife, Fanni (they were married in August 1935), by freelance commissions in translating, occasional tutoring, and assistance from his family. But it was during these few years that he published four collections of his mature poetry: *Lábadozó szél (Convalescent Wind,* 1933), *Újhold (New Moon,* 1935), *Járkálj csak, halálraítélt! (Walk on, Condemned!,* 1936), and *Meredek út (Steep Road,* 1938). In the spring of 1936 he became acquainted with Attila József, and they became close friends.

In December 1938, in recognition of his achievement in *Walk on, Condemned!,* Miklós Radnóti was awarded the prestigious Baumgarten Prize in Poetry, and after this one triumph the end came fast. Between September 1940 and the date of his death he was drafted no less than three times to serve with forced labor brigades, twice in Transylvania. On his return from his first tour of duty, on 1 November 1941, he participated in a major public demonstration, at the tombs of Lajos Kossuth and Mihály Táncsics, protesting Hungary's involvement in the war on the side of the Axis. (A similar demonstration engaged him again on 15 March of the following year.) In May 1944 he was summoned for a third and last time and taken to Bor, Yugoslavia, where he worked in the copper mines and on road construction. In the fall of that year, in the course of the general retreat of Axis forces from Eastern Europe, his unit was driven west on a forced march, and in November, in the vicinity of Abda (near Győr), the prisoners were shot and buried in a mass grave. On exhumation of the poet's remains in 1946 there was found in his field jacket a small Serbian exercise book containing ten last texts of poems written, in pencil, during his internment at the forced labor camp (at "Lager Heidenau," as most of the poems identify it). The contents of this manuscript (reproduced below in its entirety, beginning with "Seventh Eclogue") have been published in a posthumous volume, *Tajtékos ég (Sky with Clouds,* 1946), in seven editions of the poetry between 1948 and 1966, and in 1974 in facsimile, with an essay by Gyula Ortutay, under the title *Bori notesz (Bor Notebook).*

11

A poet who in a lifetime as brief as that of Mozart published literally nothing more than six slim volumes of verse, would already be putting in a claim to be considered a major author, provided that his work was of the quality of Radnóti's. The fact that Radnóti's total output numbers seventeen volumes, and that, besides poetry, he also published criticism, autobiography, children's books, and a prodigious amount of translation (see the bibliography at the end of this introduction) does more, however, than simply help increase our estimate of him as a writer even further. His translations, not excluding the version of *Don Quixote* (n.d.) or the volume, *Karunga, Lord of the Dead,* his collection of African folk tales (1944), both of them for children, show omnivorous reading, and provide us with invaluable clues to the development of the poet's sympathies. Here is where the roots of Radnóti's feeling for the unity of life and letters, his "engaged craft," lie. The subtitle of his 1943 volume of collected translations, *In Orpheus' Footsteps: Translations from Poets of Two Thousand Years,* is no exaggeration. Unlike Weöres, Radnóti does not translate from Oriental languages, and he does not, unlike József, appear interested in other East European traditions, for purposes of translation, at least (although we do know, from the instructions prefacing the *Bor Notebook,* that he knew Serbo-Croatian). But within his chosen domain: classical antiquity and the West, Radnóti offers us memorable translations from almost all the major traditions. There are poems by Greek and Latin poets (Sappho, Anacreon, Asclepiades; Vergil, Horace, the elegiac poets, Martial), by Elizabethans and English romantics (Shakespeare, Ben Jonson; Blake, Wordsworth, Byron, Shelley, Keats, Browning), by French poets since the Pléïade (Ronsard, du Bellay, de Bergerac, La Fontaine; Nerval, Mallarmé, Rimbaud; Jammes, Apollinaire, Max Jacob; Larbaud, Cendrars, Eluard, Cocteau), finally by German poets of all major periods (Kürenberg, Walther von der Vogelweide, Hadlaub; Goethe, Schiller, Hölderlin; Mörike, Keller, Meyer; Trakl, Morgenstern, Rilke, Goll, Brecht). La Fontaine's fables were of special interest to Radnóti (a volume of translations dates from 1943), and, in collaboration with his friend and fellow poet, István Vas, Radnóti was the first to publish a volume of translations from the work of Apollinaire (1940), thus securing the importance of the latter for Hungarian poetry since the twenties.

There is no question that important guiding lights of Radnóti the poet are to be found among principal enthusiasms of Radnóti the translator. Critics are generally agreed on the primacy of Vergil, Horace, Ronsard, La Fontaine, Goethe, the German romantics, and Apollinaire. It is difficult to miss the importance of Vergil for Radnóti's series of "Eclogues," Ronsard's and du Bellay's patronage of a distinguished body of work in Alexandrines, or Apollinaire's invitations to subtlety of tone, grotesquery and dry humor, formal innovation, and the cultivation of a cubist's sense of the simultaneity of times and places. But important clues too close to material encouragement do not stop where we can no longer refer to connections between translation and original work. Especially since *New Moon* Radnóti's work is alive with allusions to the work of poets whom he very probably read, but whom he never appears to have translated. Among these "submerged inspirations" are almost without a doubt Baudelaire, García Lorca, Heine, Brentano, and Hofmannsthal. Among American poets he would certainly have known Whitman, although, regrettably enough, probably not Hart Crane; the affinity with Crane is strong in places. Affinity rather than the likelihood of influence also encourages mention of Mandelstam, if only because of the strongly Mandelstamian image of the sun's wearing a hat at the end of the poem "Winter Sunshine."

The question of influence, direct or indirect, and of affinity, also applies, of course, to Radnóti's native heritage. Petőfi and other major romantics such as János Arany (1817-1882) and Mihály Vörösmarty (1800-1855) are to be sure authors from whose work every schoolboy has to memorize stretches almost as long as from the classics (at least this was true in Radnóti's lifetime). He seems also to have been well acquainted with an older writer like the language reformer Ferenc Kazinczy (1759-1831). Among contemporaries whom he knew or who were otherwise important for him, Mihály Babits, Hungary's foremost translator of Dante, occupies perhaps first place. Personal acquaintances also include the poet and novelist Dezső Kosztolányi (1885-1936), Attila József, the Catholic poet Sándor Sík (1889-1963), and István Vas. The poet's circle of acquaintances was, of course, much larger than these few names suggest; here we must confine ourselves to figures who in one way or another emerge in the poetry. Going from the metropolitan setting implied by Radnóti's fellow poets to nature and rural life, which he also loved, we may finally mention that he was strongly influenced by folk song (and by the music of his favorite composer, Béla Bartók) in much of the work not directly of a classical or Western European orientation.

Three categories of influence are attested in the mature poetry, here mentioned in order from most to least obvious. Into the first belong the rather frequent allusions to poets in titles ("Henri Barbusse Is Dead"), in dedications ("Dream Landscape / *To the memory of Clemens Brentano*"), in explanatory captions ("Song about Death / *At the funeral of Dezső Kosztolányi*"), in epigraphs (the "First Eclogue" bears a quotation from Vergil's *Georgics*), or in the text itself (in "While Writing" Kazinczy is being addressed; "Il faut laisser ..." contains a quotation from

13

Ronsard; and "First Eclogue" [1938] mourns Federico García Lorca and Attila József, both recently dead). The second, somewhat more subtle, category includes instances of indirect allusion to Radnóti's poets, either by a powerful image (as when "Chartres" recalls Rilke's sonnet cycle, or when the line "The wind steps into a puddle" ["Changing Landscape"] recalls similar conceits in Heine or in Goll), or by metrical equivalence. Here we must remember that Hungarian sources certainly helped hone Radnóti's ear, both to the intricacies of classical prosody (Vörösmarty's epic, *Zalán futása* [*Zalán's Flight*], is in dactylic hexameters) and to neoclassical and baroque poetics (Arany's epic trilogy *Toldi* is written in trochaic hexameters with a medial caesura, an ancient Hungarian meter mildly reminiscent of the Alexandrine). The importance of Vergil nevertheless remains inestimable for Radnóti's poetic self-definition (see also IV below), and critics have also stressed the formative influence of Horace. It is surprising, and to an extent regrettable, that Radnóti did not try his hand at the meters of Horace beyond two poems, "In a Restless Hour" (written in Alcaics) and "Like Death" (in a meter devised by Radnóti, combining features of the Fourth Asclepiadean and Sapphic stanzas).

Examples of the third category of influence, subtle echoes in philosophy, attitude, tone, and verbal texture, are perhaps the most difficult to identify, but they are also the most interesting. The poem "End-of-October Hexameters," which wears its prosody on its sleeve, as it were, contains some beautiful imagery, but it is at once deepened and made more exciting by our realization that in the nocturnal mood there is subtle interplay of both the Provençal *aubade* and Goethe's *Roman Elegies* (of Goethe's cycle Radnóti translated numbers 8 and 9). No less intriguing in this respect is the poem "Suddenly," whose tone bears the stamp of poets like Eluard and Brecht. There is a Brecht-like ferocity, almost reminding us of the *Moritat* of Mack the Knife in the *Three-Penny Opera,* in especially the second stanza of "Suddenly," describing an electrocution in a prison of unspecified location: "mum's the word for a bulb, a shadow runs through a cell, / and now the guards, the inmates, the worms know it's burned / human flesh they smell." In marked contrast to this aggressive tone is the tender voice in "Go to Sleep," whose warmth and alert concern with suffering, no matter where it may take place, asks to be compared with similar concern in Hofmannsthal's poem "Manche freilich ..." ("Many, of course, ..."). In the poem by Hofmannsthal the fates of those who must spend their lives in heavy labor are contrasted with the lives of the privileged. The latter are bound to the former by laws both cosmic and human: "I cannot dismiss from my eyelids / the wearinesses of wholly forgotten peoples, / nor keep away from my frightened soul / the mute plunging of distant stars."

14

Radnóti writes: "Shanghai or Guernica / are every bit as close to my heart / as is your trembling hand / or, up there somewhere, the planet Jupiter!" Most telling perhaps is an example of influence in which echoes of attitude and verbal texture ally themselves with echoes in prosody. Gyula Ortutay, in his earlier appreciation, "Radnóti Miklós" *(Kortárs* 3 [1959]: 651-64), points to the very convincing possibility that "Forced March," the penultimate Bor poem, may have been modeled on the somber rhythms of Walther von der Vogelweide's famous "Elegy," which Radnóti translated: "Oh grief, where have my years   all disappeared and gone!" Ortutay writes: "... who does not hear the melody of the *Nibelungenlied*-strophe and its painfully enclitic remembrance of home and landscapes forever past?" (p. 658), and quotes the following passages (here in my translation), from Walther's "Elegy":

> Those who were once my playmates   are tired now and old;
> here they have hewn a forest   and harvested the field,

and from "Forced March":

> his house wall lies supine;   your plum tree, broken clear,
> and all the nights back home   horripilate with fear.

The essential difference is one of intensification in tone. What begins in Walther as the expression of a traditional sensibility ends, in Radnóti, as a listing of the abhorrent specifics of a dying world.

III

The last two instances of influence cited in the preceding section, in which we overhear echoes of two poets as remote in time as Hugo von Hofmannsthal (1874-1929) and Walther von der Vogelweide (c. 1170-1228), suggest both Radnóti's unconcern with such particulars as space and time, and his intense lifelong dedication to the unity of moral sensibility and poetic craftsmanship, to quote the closing stanza of "May Picnic": "that portion of the mind / worthy of men" (see also Ortutay, p. 664). Certainly the mature Radnóti knew no higher ideal in art. Starting from only rarely doubt-ridden early attempts and ending with the clear, unyielding voice of the last poems we see this vision of unity realized in a steady progression. Few besides his friend József saw so well as Radnóti did the lot of worker and peasant under a callous and indifferent régime, but, unlike József, he also had opportunity as a student, during his "Reichenberg" period, to become acquainted with the problems of those many whom in a number of early poems

15

he calls "the proletarians" and "my brothers." Such rhetoric is soon combined with sensuous nature and love imagery and, more important, comes to exist side by side with hard, compressed language depicting industry and labor (as in "Poem of Poverty and Hate" and in "C. Neumann & Söhne"). In the early books up to and including *Song of Modern Shepherds* there is also some excellent poetry portraying the lives of country people. In "Elegy, or Icon, Nailless" a poor ne'er-do-well named John ("He [like John the Baptist, who also lived in a wilderness] is John, too") is run over by a car owned by a count, and is crippled: "Work is out of the question, so is drifting; / with wretched lawsuit-paperwork he goes hungrily / from office to office because the count / won't pay for arm, eye, or pharmacist." But a few moments of tenderness that even "John" can recollect help relieve the brutality to some extent, and the ultimate tone in the poem seems to be one of reconciliation.

Radnóti would have been very unhappy with a recent caveat in a handbook of writing, warning young poets to shy away from using what is reported in the news. The media were always important for the poet, and it was without a doubt his luck that Horthy's press was, at least relatively and for a time, truthful, especially concerning events that took place very far away. It is also significant that he had a chance to travel. What more appropriate source of poetry than "that awful paper" ("Cartes Postales") for a poet for whom the Japanese attack on Shanghai and Hitler's bombing of Guernica are every bit as vital as is the trembling hand of his beloved? In *Convalescent Wind,* centrally in the nine-poem cycle "Male Diary" (of which the poem celebrating his trial is the third), he concentrates on news events outside Hungary, at times clarifying his intent with a caption. Here is the caption to "24 April 1932" (subtitled *"John Love, My Brother"):* "During a reading of his poetry in New York's black quarter, St. Vincent, in the King White Theater, John Love, young black poet, was beaten to death onstage by Ku Klux Klan men and his body thrown out the ventilating window. All trace of the culprits was lost." The poem opens: "John Love, my brother! / Today I saw you whirling on the Tisza / under the bridge." The journalistic stance, not the energy, soon yields, in *Convalescent Wind* and in the three books following, to less time-bound expressions of interest in the faraway, in such poems as "Song of the Black Man Who Went to Town," "Montenegro Elegy," "Fire Hymn / *Variant on an African Negro Poem,"* "An Eskimo Thinks of Death," "War Diary," and "Hymn to the Nile." Among poems translated here, "Go to Sleep" is perhaps an initial focal point on these various positions, and the first two "Eclogues" and "Friday" continue to insist on the inner connectedness of public and private suffering. And everywhere the poet shows a power of evoking distant events by

16

means of sharp and clear imagery, whether those events take place close by: "Are you alive? who would know? I don't myself any more; have / stopped getting angry when, waving, they painfully cover their faces, / knowing nothing" ("Fifth Eclogue"), or far away: "Yesterday the Japanese infantry / crossed the stream Wusung, / and the thick dew of artillery blazes / its trail on Chinese meadows" ("17 February 1932 / *Peace dissolves at a whistle!*").

Events of the heart are also events, as Radnóti well knew; the themes of love and friendship are at the very core of his best work. Those various discrete celebrations of friends, mostly fellow poets, mentioned earlier, are only one light ray' rebounding from this facet of his creativity; far more impressive is the best love poetry. There are a great many bright pieces guiding us from the youthful poet's celebrations of frank sexuality ("Love Poem in the Forest" is a good example of the kind of language for which his 1931 volume was banned) to the somewhat more elevated diction of the finest love lyrics celebrating his marriage to Fanni ("Similes," "Hesitant Ode"), whom some of the most memorable poems also call by name ("In My Memories ... ," "Forced March"). Some of them most movingly demonstrate the very conditions of Radnóti's conception of love as well, what for want of a better term is here called the "threatened idyllic setting." "End-of-October Hexameters," for example, recreates a life in which nature itself gives indications both of the gathering storm of war ("corners of huge fall sky are already abloom with the blackness") and of the almost defiant security of private existence with the loved one, however modest and care-ridden their life together may be. The "Third Eclogue," in which desire to write of the beauty of the beloved is touchingly portrayed, is possibly the perfect example of the poem in which the threatened idyllic setting as poetic locus comes to life. The poet speaks to his "pastoral Muse," who will please join him in his sleepy café, among noisy salesmen and cigar-puffing lawyers, and be the poet's tutor while, outdoors, the good spring light is flying. Many of the poems end, in contrast, on the imagery of darkness or on colors suggesting death and dissolution. "In My Memories ... ," which evokes, in a middle stanza, "Fanni, in whose blue eyes passed / the landscape," along with "dear, good Paris" of the old days, ends on the image of silver clouds dissolving overhead. In Radnóti's poetry the color silver, according to a recent study of the color imagery by Marianna D. Birnbaum *(Irodalomtörténeti Közlemények [Papers in Literary History]* 78 [1974]: 703-05), symbolizes death, along with the white of moonlight ("The Terrible Angel") and of decay ("Root"). Related to these colors is the flavor bitter, and the bitterness of feeling, of the essential homelessness of the poet who should be a source of joy to others and yet whom no one needs. The tones of many of the later poems preoccupied with the exile condition of the poet are alternately bitter and bittersweet, thus tying together themes and feelings of love and desperation. Birnbaum points especially to "Winter Sunday" as a poem which starts with gold and ends on silver (pp. 703-04), but a partial reverse progression, as in "Sky with Clouds," is equally effective.

IV

Any general introduction to Radnóti's poetry must devote some time to his stately series of "Eclogues," considered by many Hungarian critics to be the pinnacle of the poet's achievement. My qualified agreement with this view (a share of top honors should go to the Bor poetry) has led me to translate the entire series in this volume, including "Spring Is in Flight," subtitled *'Preface to the Eclogues.'* For some reason, having presumably to do with the shortness of the imprisoned poet's memory, a "Sixth Eclogue" is missing from the series, and no poem between the "Fifth" and "Seventh" is a likely candidate on formal grounds alone (all of Radnóti's known "Eclogues" are in hexameters or in dialogue, or in both). But the existing series is so dignified and so complete that the business of numbering is of little importance. The most understandable questions that we are likely to ask: Why the eclogue form; what does Radnóti need Vergil's world for? are the ones that critics on the home front have been puzzling over. The most useful answers stress the importance simultaneously of kinship and of contrast. Vergil's world is as different from Radnóti's as it is similar to it; it is idyllic and threatened by turns; and the depiction of modern suffering and the plight of war lends Radnóti's voice an edge and a psychological depth which contemporary poetry in classical meters seldom if ever has. It is in the very act of borrowing a manner that the modern poet is innovative. Especially in the "First," "Second," "Fourth," and "Eighth," the poems in dialogue, the avant-garde poetics shines: to tremendous effect the poet's voice breaks in two. It carries on a conversation with itself; whether the "Poet" persona's interlocutor is cast as "Shepherd," as "Pilot," as "Voice," or as "Prophet," the speakers in the tiny duodrama play a *Doppelgänger* game of psychic chance. The outward "answers" are never beyond either the poet's reach or ours, be the occasion for meeting and talking the horrors of the Spanish Civil War and the deaths of Lorca and József ("First Eclogue"), the Allied bombing raids on Hungarian cities ("Second" and "Eighth"), or the survival of the poet and of his voice ("Fourth"). What the poet risks is a possible misunderstanding. There has been some comment in the scholarship on the sensibility that at times unabashedly portrays lounging in sun and air, among peaceful

18

shepherds and shepherdess muses. But the misunderstanding is all too soon cleared up; the poet wins at his dice. The "pedestrian shuffle" of the maker of idylls is immediately confronted by the athletic walk of the angry communist poet, and the two movements are, as it were, synthesized in the transcendent choreography of literary borrowing and repayment. The idyllic setting and the idyll itself are threatened without relief; the balance in feeling is always precarious and delicate.

The question, then, What does Radnóti need Vergil for? is at least in part answered within the necessities of literary tradition, within which a poet, whatever else he may need to do with his energies, adopts an ancient model, finally to transform it into an idea completely his own. But the modern poet's choice is not an arbitrary one; he may feel affinity with his *miglior fabbro* even prior to demonstrable influence. After all, Vergil too was a "war poet." He too lived in turbulent times, and he is also concerned with the threatened idyllic existence (as evident, for example, in the *Ninth Eclogue,* which Radnóti translated). A textual comparison between Vergil's *Ninth* and Radnóti's "First" should no doubt prove instructive. It is also true that direct hints of Vergil's guiding presence are nowhere far in Radnóti's own series. To mention only three: there are the epigraph from the *Georgics* heading the "First" and the conceit of the "pastoral Muse" throughout the "Third" (both mentioned above); most interesting perhaps, and the most characteristically Vergilian hint of all, there is the mention of the "rabbi," an intimation of Christ, in the "Eighth." The soundness of this last parallel does, however, depend on the quality of the messianic interpretation so often given by interested classicists to the image of Pollio's newborn son in Vergil's *Fourth Eclogue.* Quite apart from this last point, these presences in Radnóti's "Eclogues" are never mere embellishments, and Vergil is not a persona in even a Poundian sense. Rather, the Latin poet offers the Hungarian a firm foundation for his very poetic being, a foundation whose validity endures to the end. Nowhere need this be more deeply sensed than in the increasing perfection of the dactylic hexameter, which Radnóti clearly favors, and which he uses as many times outside the "Eclogues" as within them (e.g. "Night," "To a Poetaster"). In the end the utter naturalness and lightness of the poet's handling of the meter (to which his language is, to be sure, eminently suited), as in "Seventh Eclogue," are surely a part of that mastery which is the poet's alone, and which nowadays is rarely attempted, let alone attained, by anyone except possibly Weöres.

The stress on Vergil's tutoring hand should not make us inattentive to the "Eclogues" not in hexameter, the "Second" and the "Fourth." Both are interesting, the "Second" because of its rhymed six-footers and thus Racine-like ring, the "Fourth" because of its sensitively modulated language. In the latter the lines

19

"Help me, liberty, / let me find my true home at last" may strike us as garishly resembling Petőfi at some of the romantic poet's worst. But the opening exchange of speeches, on birth and health, is effective, and the line: "And the horrible flower / cancer is not yet blossoming in your flesh" especially so when it is read against Radnóti's poem in memory of Babits, who died of cancer ("Only Skin and Bones and Pain"). The line from the "Fourth": "Death already whistles among the trees" could not be more powerful in bringing to mind the closing line of "Picture Postcards" number 3: "Death blows overhead, revolting."

V

The crown jewels of Radnóti's work, the most publicized and, in a sense which is valid critically, the most moving phase, are the poems of the *Bor Notebook.* Here the poet reveres to the last the law of the unity of form and meaning, and he enforces it within himself, as it were, in a world which at that very moment is opting for the formless and the irrational. As much as this happens in the best holocaust literature (if we wish to call the contents of the *Notebook* that), we overhear in these poems at least a whisper of the Socratic dictum that injustice, when taken in the right spirit, cannot make us worse human beings, that is, cannot deprive our lives of meaning or reduce us to formlessness. We do hear a cry *de profundis,* the voice of a man suffering from sickness and homesickness, and in a state of transfiguring confrontation with death. But the cry is gentle and urbane, and the suffering is objectified in some of the most vital concerns that we share with the imprisoned poet. It has been suggested that the lexicon of the "Dungeon" scene at the end of Goethe's *Faust, Part I* is a reservoir of all the important vocabulary of the preceding twenty scenes, the tragedy of Margaret. In much the same way the Bor poetry, this "dungeon scene" of the drama of Radnóti's career, gathers up the threads of major themes of the foregoing books: love ("Letter to My Wife"), home ("Seventh Eclogue," "Forced March"), friendship ("À la recherche ..."), man's sense of rootedness in nature and his eventual dissolution and rebirth in it ("Root"), the poet's fascination with the apocalypse of war and with innocent but doomed attempts at ongoing normal life ("Picture Postcards"), among others. The essentially saintly moral posture, unaffected and unwavering to the end, can also be expressed in negatives. Nowhere does Radnóti accuse, or blame Hungarians for the Nazi horrors, and many would agree that in this he is generous to a fault. Nowhere does he indulge in self-pity; *nowhere does he recant.* We never sense that he is letting his poetic persona imitate the posture of personal regret; had the poet only been more submissive, or more prudent, or more ener-

20

getic in attempts to escape, he would not now be in the predicament in which he and others are finding themselves. The survival of the individual matters less than the survival of a voice. This is clearly discernible also from the fact that he gives, on the first leaf of his *Lager* notebook, detailed instructions in five languages to "its finder," asking said person to deliver it to Ortutay, and that he allows fellow campmates to make copies of the poems. Nowhere does Radnóti subscribe to the view, so often heard in the Hungary of his day: *Inter arma silent Musae.* Quite the contrary: it was all the antecedents of the war and the war itself that made him the poet that he in the end became.

Most intriguing of all, perhaps, although not totally surprising: Radnóti does not stress, he does not even mention, his Jewishness. This is admittedly no surprise after the examples of Canetti, Celan, Mandelstam, and Brodsky, although others, notably Nelly Sachs (who, for one, was spared), were of a diametrically opposed orientation. It is much emphasized in the growing literature that Radnóti was so assimilated a Jew that he was more Hungarian than his "indigenous" compatriots themselves. In this too he was not unique. He counted among his closest friends Jew and non-Jew alike, no less than persons of every political bent, on both left and right. (This seems clear from "À la recherche ... ," where in stanza 4 he concedes the right of the last chauvinist to fight for the cause he believes in.) The religious side of his "Jewish identity" is somewhat more complicated. The religiosity that shines forth in his poetry has been the subject of some controversy. In the early books there is a "pagan piety" that makes frequent use of references to icons, Christ-child images, crucifixes, saints, and the like, and often combines such imagery with erotic language. On a perhaps more academic and "serious" plane, poems such as "Marginal Note to the Prophet Habakkuk" and "Eighth Eclogue" also leave no doubt that Radnóti knew his Bible. Although this is not directly pertinent to the Bor poems, the marvelous mythopoeia in "Columbus" deserves mention here: it takes no more than freeing of "a dove" in line 11 to conjure a mental image of Noah's Ark; see also the overt mention of Noah but three poems over, in the closing line of "Paris." On the basis of such evidence it seems useful to suggest that Radnóti was a man and poet religious in the most humane sense, possessed of a cosmic awareness to which neither sectarian persuasions nor official dogmas of any description have much relevance.

The most moving instance of the poet's cosmic and humane vision comes, appropriately enough, at the end. In "Eighth Eclogue," in conversation with the prophet Nahum, returned across the ages to witness the horrors visited upon the present, there comes through a prophetic reinterpretation of modern man's folly and plight. The poet remains sanguine, despite everything that he has been through,

21

that there is enough humanity left in the world and enough responsiveness to the peculiar rage of poets to help realize that "kingdom ... which a certain youthful disciple had promised: / rabbi, who came and fulfilled our law and the word of the prophets." In this synthesis of the Jewish, the Christian, and the classical, we have an epiphany in three distinct senses. First, there is a purely aesthetic *stretto maestrale* effect reminiscent of the broken-off surprise ending (where the composer died) of J. S. Bach's final work, *The Art of the Fugue.* Second, we have a synthesis in the poetic vision of cultures that challenges comparison with the reconciliation of the Christian and the Hellenic which Hölderlin achieves in his hymn "Patmos." And third and most central: we witness a culmination in the unity of poetic being in the essential Radnótian sense, a sense from which the poet never wavered, once he had made it his own during the few years of maturity that were given him.

VI

Radnóti is not an easy poet to translate, that is, to translate well. We could do worse than listen to the poet's own lines on the subject of poiesis (from "Second Eclogue"): "And how filled a poem is with danger, / if you knew: how delicate a single line is, what a stranger / in its moods!" and on translation (from that perhaps problematic statement, the afterword to *In Orpheus' Footsteps*):

> The translating poet knows that it is not possible to "translate" a foreign poem; it is possible only to write it anew, and that all translation is — experiment. And he also knows that, with few exceptions, there is no foreign poem that could not be translated ... . You just have to have a bit of Orpheus in you to do it, because Orpheus was a magician, among other things, ... And — and you need luck to bring it off.

The reason I undertook this translation project, in the fall of 1974, was an almost personal feeling that Radnóti deserves an English-speaking audience, and my realization that hitherto available translations into English are unsatisfactory at best. I have seen work by four or five translators, in journals, including *The New Hungarian Quarterly* (published in Budapest), which latter regularly prints good Hungarian poetry in English translations of mixed quality, and in one volume (published by Harper & Row in 1972), which, if I may say so, is an extremely slipshod piece of work. Contrary to the fact that looseness, sloppiness, contempt for prosodic and formal values is very much the fashion in some quarters in contemporary poetry, such an approach to Radnóti does not serve either his spirit

22

or his practical poetics, and there is, hearteningly enough, a direction in American verse which does encourage the crafted and the sensitively precise. I hope I am right in thinking that my work takes up camp on this side.

In the fifty poems that follow I have aimed first and foremost at fidelity, in form, pattern, diction, tone, mood, prosody, down to sound repetitions and to junctural and other suprasegmental suggestions. My attempts to reach the versions I wanted were not, of course, without their setbacks. One of the handicaps under which an American translator of poetry in classical meters labors is a widespread misconception concerning the fighting chance that certain meters have (according to the misconception: do not have) in English. This comes through in the practically expressed attitudes of some eminent classicist-poets. Richmond Lattimore, for example, shies away from hexameters in his *Iliad* (unless the line hits upon the pattern by accident), but he translates a sonnet by Ronsard into Alexandrines worthy of the original ("When You Are Old: After Ronsard," *The Hudson Review* 23 [Winter 1970-71]: 671). I, for one, am a firm believer in hexameters in English, whether dactylic or iambic, and have in this regard preferred to follow poets and translators such as W. H. Auden, John Hollander, and Daryl Hine. The beautifully effortless hexameters in Daryl Hine's translation of the *Homeric Hymns* should help convince any halfway sympathetic reader that English does have a sufficient tradition in classical prosodies to justify faithful translation of poetry in such meters. I can only hope that my own meters and rhythms, tones and sonorities will manage, in ways that show respect toward the English language, to suggest something of the grace, fluidity, and power of Radnóti's originals.

Any comparison of translations with their originals must bring up at least a question or two concerning the relation of source language to target. Hungarian could not be more different from English if it were Sumerian. Like the latter, Hungarian is both non-Indo-European and agglutinative; it works with suffixes rather than with prepositions, and can thus manage to say what an English line or sentence says, in less physical space. Another important difference is that, while in Hungarian there are no prepositions in the literal sense (all such adverbials are postpositive), all modifiers of a substantive precede it. Thus slow and careful untangling of a long modifier or series of modifiers in the course of translation feels akin to the word-by-word retrograde decoding of a text, vaguely similar to a beginner's trying to get used to reading a modern Semitic language. One excellent, although by no means uncommon, example of this "retrograde effect" was felt in translating the compressed industry poem "C. Neumann & Söhne." To convey the effect, let me quote a few lines in the original, followed by the translation; the numbers indicate corresponding words (lines 14-17):

$$\overset{1}{...}\ \overset{2}{és}\ \overset{}{t\ddot{o}bb}\ a\ \overset{3}{forg\acute{o},}$$

$$\overset{4}{cs\ddot{o}p\ddot{o}g\H{o}}\ \overset{5}{tengelyek}\ \overset{6}{k\ddot{o}z\ddot{o}tt}\ \overset{7}{fogantyúk}$$

$$\overset{8}{után}\ \overset{9}{kapaszkodó}\ \overset{10}{gépész}\ \overset{11}{halálos}$$

$$\overset{12}{lihegésénél},\ ...\ .$$

In English this reads (lines 14-16):

$$\overset{1}{...}\ \overset{2}{and\ more}\ than\ the\ \overset{11}{deathly}\ \overset{12}{panting}$$

$$of\ the\ \overset{10}{machinist,}\ \overset{9}{grasping}\ \overset{8}{after}\ \overset{7}{handgrips}$$

$$\overset{6}{among}\ the\ \overset{3}{revolving,}\ \overset{4}{dripping}\ \overset{5}{axles},\ ...\ .$$

In the selection below all seven of Radnóti's volumes of verse, including, of course, the posthumous *Sky with Clouds,* are represented. At least one or two poems are included from every book (as indicated in the Table of Contents), and, as mentioned earlier, I did include poems connected with his confiscation trial. I have also attempted, where this was practicable, to show the marvelous balanc‐ ing effect of some of the earlier versus the later poetry. But in my overall choices I was guided not by such external considerations but by literary merit. On that count alone I wish there were the room to accommodate another fifty poems. I would have liked, for example, to translate more of the "Reichenberg" poetry, or more of the early "country folk" lyric, or *all* of *Sky with Clouds.*

In closing I would like to state that I have done all of the translating myself. Despite some good results in the field of team translating, I frankly distrust collaborations between nonpoet speakers and nonspeaker poets. That which is proverbially "lost in translation" can always be depended on to be lost, no matter what the working arrangement. But that which we stand to gain through this work can, I believe, be gained best if the same mind is competent both to perceive the originals and to make their equivalents. Although, as I have said, I can but hope that these translations will do honor to the growing reputation of a major contem‐ porary, and while there is no doubt always some room for improvement, I have found, to my own satisfaction at least, that Radnóti's poetry repays solitary work. I thank the interested reader and wish him much enjoyment.

MIKLÓS RADNÓTI: SELECT BIBLIOGRAPHY

Note: This bibliography is limited to first editions of Radnóti's works, and to sources used in the preparation of the present volume.

1. First Editions of Radnóti's Works *(see also Tezla, pp. 482-83)*

Naptár. [*Calendar.* (Poems)] Budapest: Hungaria, 1924.

Pogány köszöntő. [*Pagan Salute.* (Poems)] Budapest: Kortárs, 1930.

Újmódi pásztorok éneke. [*Song of Modern Shepherds.* (Poems)] Budapest: Fiatal Magyarország, 1931.

Lábadozó szél. [*Convalescent Wind.* (Poems)] Szeged: Szegedi Fiatalok Művészeti Kollégiuma, 1933.

Ének a négerről, aki a városba ment. S. Szőnyi Lajos 20 linómetszetével. [*Song of the Black Man Who Went to Town.* With 20 linocuts by Lajos S. Szőnyi. (Separate chapbook edition of the poem)] Budapest: Gyarmati, 1934.

Kaffka Margit művészi fejlődése. [*The Artistic Development of Margit Kaffka.* (Dissertation)] Szeged: Szegedi Fiatalok Művészeti Kollégiuma, 1934.

Újhold. [*New Moon.* (Poems)] Szeged: Szegedi Fiatalok Művészeti Kollégiuma, 1935.

Járkálj csak, halálraítélt! [*Walk on, Condemned!* (Poems)] Budapest: Nyugat, 1936.

Meredek út. [*Steep Road.* (Poems)] Budapest: Cserépfalvi, 1938.

Cervantes: Don Quijote. Radnóti Miklós átdolgozásában. [In the reworked version by M. R.] Budapest: Cserépfalvi, n.d.

Guillaume Apollinaire válogatott versei. Fordítás. Vas Istvánnal. [*Selected Poems of G. A.* Translation. With I. V.] Budapest, 1940.

Ikrek hava. [*Önéletrajzi emlékezések*] [*Month of Twins. (Autobiographical Memoirs)*] Budapest: Almanach, 1940.

Válogatott versek. [*Selected Poems*] 1930-1940. Budapest: Almanach, 1940.

J. de la Fontaine: Válogatott mesék. [Fordítás] [*J. de la F.: Selected Fables* (Translation)] Budapest, 1943.

Huizinga válogatott tanulmányai. [*Selected Essays of (Jan) Huizinga* (Translation)] Budapest: Pharos, 1943.

Orpheus nyomában: Műfordítások kétezer év költőiből. [Képes Gézával, Szemlér Ferenccel és Vas Istvánnal] [*In Orpheus' Footsteps: Translations from Poets of Two Thousand Years* (With G. K., F. Sz., and I. V.)] Budapest: Pharos, 1943.

Karunga, a holtak ura: Néger népmesegyűjtemény. [*Karunga, Lord of the Dead: Collection of Negro Folk Tales*] Budapest: Pharos, 1944.

Tajtékos ég. [Versek] [*Sky with Clouds.* (Poems)] Budapest: Révai, 1946.

2. Later Editions; Biography; Translation

Radnóti Miklós összes versei és műfordításai. [Szerkesztette Réz Pál] [*Complete Poems and Translations of M. R.* (Edited by P. R.)] Budapest: Magyar Helikon, 1966.
The edition used in preparing the translations in this volume.

Radnóti Miklós 1909-1944. Szerkesztette Baróti Dezső. A Petőfi Irodalmi Múzeum kiadványai, 4. [*M. R. 1909-1944.* Edited by D. B. Publications of the Petőfi Museum of Literature, 4.] Budapest: Magyar Helikon, 1959.

Radnóti Miklós. Bori notesz. [Hasonmás kiadás, szerkesztette Szántó Tibor és Réz Pál. Harmadik kiadás] [*M. R. Bor Notebook.* (Facsimile edition, edited by T. Sz. and P. R. Third Printing)] Budapest: Magyar Helikon, 1974.
In two small volumes: (1) facsimile, (2) transcription and notes, prefaced by an essay by Gyula Ortutay.

Miklós Radnóti. Clouded Sky. Translated from the Hungarian by Steven Polgar, Stephen Berg, S. J. Marks. New York: Harper & Row, 1972.
The only previous American translation of Radnóti's poetry. Contains text of 1946 volume. Out of print.

3. Secondary Sources

Birnbaum, Marianna D. "Radnóti színei" [R.'s Colors], *Irodalomtörténeti Közlemények* [*Papers in Literary History*] 78 (1974): 701-06.

Molnár, Ferenc. "Radnóti Miklós pályakezdésének körülményeiről" [On Circumstances Surrounding the Beginning of M. R.'s Career], *Irodalomtörténeti Közlemények* 72 (1968): 343-49.

Ortutay, Gyula. "Radnóti Miklós" [M. R.], *Kortárs* [*Contemporary*] 3 (1959): 651-64. [Reprinted as introductory essay in Baróti, pp. 5-33]

Sőtér, István. "Miklós Radnóti, A Twentieth Century Poet," *The New Hungarian Quarterly* [Budapest], no. 18 (Summer 1965), pp. 3-13.

4. Handbooks

Magyar Életrajzi Lexikon. Szerkesztette Kenyeres Ágnes. [*Hungarian Biographical Dictionary.* Edited by Á. K.] 2 vols. Budapest: Akadémiai Kiadó, 1967, 1969.

Tezla, Albert. *Hungarian Authors: A Bibliographical Handbook.* Cambridge, Mass.: The Belknap Press, Harvard University Press, 1970.

SUBWAY STOPS

Ó, költő tisztán élj te most, ...

("Járkálj csak, halálraítélt!")

O poet, live a life of purity now, ...

("Walk on, Condemned!")

SUNBODIED VIRGINS, SHEPHERDS AND FLOCKS

Slowly the shepherd too comes down from the mountain;
locked into the fold, white, the flock
crowds; and sunbathed virgins also
descend from the hill, their hips rocking,
sweet-smelling, dreamily, as at each
autumn, when under the black skies the trees
die; sunbodied virgins, shepherds and flocks
come down slowly toward the village.

We too break; under our women's
mirroring eyes the shadows grow blacker,
and winter snows on us out of our kisses;
our hair too falls into our brows on the left,
and no one soothes our inflamed eyes,
only sunbodied virgins, shepherds and flocks
walk slowly down toward the village, where
sorrow is now gathering in pregnant clouds.

13 October — 24 November 1929

POEM OF POVERTY AND HATE

Brother, I've slept, nights, at the foot of
black, smokehaired firewalls with dreams
of poverty and hate, and, pockets turned inside-out,
I've screamed the song of the penniless
toward the gold-wombed furnaces!

Loving, sphere-shaped hate-words kept turning
the transmissions' slothful wheel, when filet-fleshed
white dreams got caught squeezed between belts!

My hands, with the weight of hardened workman-hands,
slapped my thighs, and I loved the factories' daughters,
who lugged autumnal armies' trembling labors
onto the mountain of poverty-hate, and my fingers,
soaking paths of the squirting oil, sticking, grasped
at nothing!

My lower eyelids were a Golgotha loaded with
wrinkles sagging under sweat-crucifixes,
where nights' coal-dust Christs loomed tight, blue.

11 October 1928

C. NEUMANN & SÖHNE

What titanic living-up, living-out it is
of every tiny life they've killed into it;
to the rhythm of the machines the factory sighs:
but it dies, evenings, when the siren starts up,
and out the gates, flung open, push
the sad, pale workers and the
girls, who from beside the oil-blooded,
death-rattling machines, ears buzzing, running,
tussling, giggling, flee to the streets,
and this scuffling, tussling means more to them
than the plant's colossally buzzing,
pulsing music; ... these tiny, minute
voices are more than the machines' dizzying
symphonies; ... and more than the deathly panting
of the machinist, grasping after handgrips
among the revolving, dripping axles,
once he sees flashing — the bloodred light
of the lamp signaling a breakdown.
What a gigantic life the sighing of the
great machines makes! and yet it's to the rhythm of
women's tiny laughter that life revolves.

Reichenberg, 17 October 1927

SATURDAY NIGHT GROTESQUE

The full moon sits on the treetop and
swings red on the branches. Piercingly a
winedrunk workman's reeling voice howls.
Bats fly between trees, and even a black-
uniformed policeman whistles his
buddy on the beat closer. From the taverns
wind starts out and builds dusttowers
on the road, where, in love, four
greyhounds the color of breakfast rolls run.
Women now fear in their homecoming men
their tense, unborn children!

Budapest, 28 September 1930

PORTRAIT, ANGRY AS HELL

Addled little poets are writing
my poems again, and beneath me
they fatten into gloomy worms!
No, not even into worms! for
all they are is fly dirt
on holy icon frames,
which the devout, at Easter
cleaning, scratch off!

Budapest, 24 January 1931

ELEGY, OR ICON, NAILLESS

He is John, too; he was bumming it on the road
without work; wandered now and then; sometimes,
resting, he counted the softening callouses on his fist,
and yawned a wet one into his palm.

Then he just kept going again, with some bread,
a gift, over his heart and, so as not to be
alone, pulled god out of the sky
by the legs, right down next to him, giving it praise
with each sprained ankle in hard, short little prayers.

And one night the count's dust-raiser of a car
caught him and flung him down; now he's one-eyed,
one-armed, lame, and not even a war casualty.

Work is out of the question, so is drifting;
with wretched lawsuit-paperwork he goes hungrily
from office to office because the count
won't pay for arm, eye, or pharmacist.

He thinks very far back: that night when they
drove him into town the count's lover
sat next to him and, white and kind of hysterical,
held his bleeding forehead with a scented scarf.

He thinks of her now and of that balladworthy
mutt who once, for a single gentle stroke of his,
wouldn't budge from his heel for three days.

13 January 1931

8 DECEMBER 1931

(Public Hearing)

For Dr. Kornél Melléky

In front of me Müller, the printer,
stood before the scales,
was weighed,
and got six months.

Then they emptied the courtroom, it being
my turn; they were guarding the public
against my contagious poems.

I felt like crackling, spitting
like a fire surrounded by desiccated men
in company with the pleasure of chattering
slabs of bacon and waiting loaves.

I would have spat like a fire who gets
only the bright drops of the bacon it
turns on itself, grinding its teeth,

but I shone nonetheless, like sleepy embers,
and they blew on me, to get me to defend myself,
because that's how it's done; and the counsel
for the prosecution blew on me: damn you, die down.

No extenuating circumstances were visible,
and two of my poems weighed in at eight days;
I heard it, standing up. They knew from whom I'd
had my birth, where and when; we knew one another,
and as they went out, they didn't even say goodbye.

I stood with my lawyer, and around me
some friends were chatting and some talespinners;
it was all of two-thirty in the afternoon,
and my sweetheart, fingers crossed, stood on the street,
her eyes getting big as wheels.

LOVE POEM IN THE FOREST

This forest is much like your obliging sweetheart
who, lying still before you, opens in two
and yet encloses you and guards your life
in a hard circle; she guards it so that, if you grew,
you could grow only upward, the way this forest
grows upward, and salutes you with its sun-hat!

And your sweetheart too is much like this forest
where, in silence stained with shadow, the resin freezes,
and yet a song-filled brightness pulls through it
when the wind awakens and blows on the leaves —
this is how love irradiates you too,
and its guarding hand shields you from thick cares!

1934

WHILE WRITING

Only a snake could fill a tree trunk with revulsion,
leaving on it his skin, the way this round revolving
world and these rotted-out men fill me with disgust.
I was born to father flowers, but then my childhood passed
among weapons and thugs. Brought up indifferent toward
having to fight, I never turned and ran, a coward.

True, it is good to let them have it now and then;
to live, that would be best — to write, to show all men.
I pour myself some courage, lest I just pack up and go;
sweet thought: to go live far away, in some studio.
I'm thinking of you now, pen in my working hand,
old master Kazinczy — I'm coming to understand.

17 March 1935

BALLAD

The murderer runs with his mouth open,
from his mouth flutters his breath.

Blood writes deep into the snow and smokes;
the ticklish knife reaches the heart of the dead.

Huddling over him bend
silent snow and gossiping wind.

1936

CHARTRES

Stone saint stirs on top of his pillar; it's eight o'clock,
the blunt light waits for the plunging dusk.
And a voice calls from on high: True, I lived in the flesh,
but it's not by flesh I saw combat and clashed.

Night eavesdrops; now the saint rejoins the ranks,
returning to dead stone. His chin is chipped.
Was it a storm or a steel-toothed pagan who took a bite?

He has vanished.
In his hand was a tablet and on his brow, the light.

1937

CARTES POSTALES

From Chartres to Paris

The lamp was blinking on the train,
the moon stuck to the flowing windows now and then;
facing me sat a soldier; on his heart
shone a blonde. She smiled; her dream was light.

Versailles

The pond boils over and its mirror snaps;
out of fat fish fall roes of eggs.
Slender girls look on, motionless,
golden drops falling on their legs.

Jardin du Luxembourg

Fresh sand is still happily flowing
between the children's grubbing fingers,
but from behind their knitting the women
busy with needles are already calling them.

Quai de Montebello

A little girl just ran by,
she held an apple in her hand.
It was a big red apple,
the little girl bent over it.
Breath lingers on the sky,
the moon is so pale.

Place de la Notre-Dame

Throw that awful paper away: Notre-Dame
is waving a cheerful cloud, white as a lamb.
Think of nothing else: sit down, look around,
observe! for tomorrow, above the square,
gray dawn will surely break without you there.

7 August — 7 September 1937

SONG ABOUT DEATH

At the funeral of Dezső Kosztolányi

Above the grave the autumn fog is sifting;
it's early yet, and see: it has turned evening.
Slowly the heavy smoke of torches weaves
on our dark sky a sterling silver wreath,

and, high above, a startled bird cries!
The soul is so quick to frighten and to fly,
just like the cool, light-wingèd cloud
breathed on by incandescent stars.

Silent, the body in its pit now rests;
down there, it lives the peaceful fate of crusts
of earth, dissolves; thirsty roots drink it up,
and with vernal splendor it returns,

according to law! and it's ghostly to have it so —
what was one world has orbited into two!
Or is it wise? The body here knows it whole.
Preserve, o Lord, the pathways of the soul.

1937

42

MARGINAL NOTE

TO THE PROPHET HABAKKUK

Cities
stood in flames,
villages
erupted!
Be with me,
strict
Habakkuk!

Cold now,
black, the
cinders;
within me
the fiery
bite
still embers!

Bitter
my drink,
my food.
Black rage —
cover me
head-to-foot
with soot!

1937

MARGINAL NOTE TO LUKE

Moonsickle
watches him
till morning,
finally
wandering
shepherds
find him.

His cradle a
manger,
radiant,
lightfilled!

Standing there, they
gape at him
out of their
blackness;
among them two
devoted cows
befog the
mirror
of the child's
glistening
skin.

20 October 1937

GO TO SLEEP

There is always a murder somewhere:
      on a valley's lap, her eyelashes
closed, or on searching mountaintops,
      anywhere; and there's no sense
in consoling me by saying it's far away!
      Shanghai or Guernica
are every bit as close to my heart
      as is your trembling hand
or, up there somewhere, the planet Jupiter!
      Don't look at the sky now,
don't look at earth, either — just sleep!
      Death has run amok in the dust
of the spark-throwing Milky Way,
      and is sprinkling the falling,
wild shades with its silver spray.

1937

IL FAUT LAISSER ...

Il faut laisser maison et vergers et jardins —
Ronsard begins one of his last poems on this line;
I murmur it to myself; the brown bridle-path listens;
from the garden's rosebushes some dead petals are flying.
Two naked bushes gaze after me, sad and spent,
it seems the whole region knows French to some extent;
il faut laisser — the oak too recites as it daydreams,
and drops a tired acorn on its steaming bed of leaves.

The sun sits among clouds; leashed on a rope, a goat
starts on a walk and trails, a bearded, white depressive,
making the rounds and dipping into the pasture's puddles;
up in squares of the sky a bird team swims in a *V,*
vanishing, off and on, in the slow twilight gray.
Among thin foliage flutters a veil of cooling rain:
il faut laisser, it whispers, they laid Ronsard to his peace;
just wait: on you too, one day, the pearling sweat will freeze.

7 October 1938

46

FIRST ECLOGUE

Quippe ubi fas versum atque nefas; tot bella per orbem,
tam multae scelerum facies; ... .

—*Vergil*

Shepherd:
Long time, no see around; have the thrushes at long last lured you?

Poet:
Listen: those woods are so full of clatter that spring must be here now!

Shepherd:
This isn't spring yet, the sky's at play; just look at that puddle:
gently it smiles at you now, but when night frost locks up its mirror,
it will sneer at you! for it's April, the fool, don't you trust him.
Poor small tulips, look at them, way over there, how they've frozen.
Say, what makes you so sad? would you like to sit down on this stone here?

Poet:
Sad is not what I'd call it. I'm used to this horrible world, so
much, there are times it's forgetting to ache any more. I'm disgusted.

Shepherd:
So then it's true that wild on the Pyrenees' peaks there are red-hot
gun-muzzles arguing right in the midst of the blood-frozen corpses,
so that the bears and soldiers flee from that chaos together;
armies of women and children and oldsters, bundles on backs, run,
slam down prone when above them death starts circling, and there are
so many dead flung about, there's no one to come to remove them.
Knowing you knew Federico, I'll ask: did he make it to safety?

Poet:
No, he did not. It's been two years now: he was killed in Granada.

Shepherd:
He ... García Lorca is dead! that no one has told me!
News of war travel fast, so fast; and the men who are poets
vanish: like that! Didn't Europe have some memorial observance?

47

Poet:
No one as much as took note. It's good if the wind pokes the embers,
finds some broken lines on the site of the pyre and learns them.
That's how much will be left of the oeuvre, for a scholarly future.

Shepherd:
Didn't escape, then; he died. Well, true: where could poets be running?
Attila József didn't escape; he kept gesturing *No* to
this, our established order, and tell me: who weeps that it killed him?
What about you? can *your* words find any echo in these times?

Poet:
Cannon rumbling? in ashen ruins, with villages plundered?
Still, I write, and I live in the midst of this mad-dog world, as
lives that oak: it knows they'll be cutting it down; that white cross
on it signals: tomorrow the tree men will buzz-saw the region,
waits for that fate; in the meantime it sprouts its new leaves regardless.
You have it good: here it's peaceful, it's seldom that even a wolf comes
your way; you're apt to forget that the flock which you tend is another's.
It's been months that even the owner has shown up around here.
Peace. By the time I get home I'll have ancient evening descending,
with that moth of sunset spraying its silvery wing dust.

1938

IN A RESTLESS HOUR

I lived high up, in winds, where the sun shone bright;
my home: your broken son's in a valley now.
    You wrap me deep in shadows, nor will
        heavenly play of the twilight soothe me.

Above me sheer cliffs, distant the brilliant sky;
I'm in the deep now, down among speechless stones.
    Shall I grow silent too? What moves your
        powers today? Is it death? Who asks it?

Who needs your detailed reckoning on your life,
or on this poem here, left in its broken state?
    Learn, then: no single sigh shall mourn you,
        no one will bury you; earth won't cradle

your dust; the winds will scatter you. Yet that cliff
will echo all — tomorrow, if not today —
    I'm telling it, and sons and daughters
        growing to wisdom will understand it.

10 January 1939

THURSDAY

In New York in a small hotel
T. tied a noose around his neck;
can a man gone homeless for so many years
continue a wandering wreck?

In Prague it was J. M. who killed himself,
he was at home and yet remained afoot;
P. R. hasn't written in a year, either,
he may be dead under a dried-out root.

He was a poet and he went to Spain,
where his eyes were clouded over by grief;
and the man, the poet who would like to be free,
should he scream before a shining knife?

May he cry out before infinity itself
when his finite road is at an end;
is a man allowed to call out for his life
when he lives without a home or is in chains?

When it's the lamb who begins to bite,
and the turtle dove who lives on bloody flesh;
when the snake whistles out on the road,
and the wind starts to scream and to lash?

26 May 1939

50

LIKE DEATH

Silence sits on my heart, covers me, lazy, dark;
silent clinking of frost; the river pops and runs
along the path in the woods; mirroring painfully, stops,
                                        stabs at its banks now.

When will this winter end? Bones of beautiful, old
lovers lie under earth, cold, and I know they'll crack.
Deep in the lap of his cave, ruffled, the grizzly bear cries,
                                        so does the deer fawn.

On the little fawn weeps; the winter sky is lead;
dancing, the clouds' talons, blown by the dark and cold;
light of the moon glints through; snow-colored fear flies about,
                                        shaking the treetops.

Slow, this game of the frost, slow and somber as death;
frail flower, made of ice, snaps on your windowpane,
just lace, would you believe, tumbling heavily downward,
                                        so many sweat beads.

So this poem of mine softly steps up to you;
quietly words knock together, take to their wings, and fall
just like death. And a rustling, and a stillness that full
                                        follow in silence.

27 February 1940

51

SKY WITH CLOUDS

The moon rocks on a sky with clouds,
I'm amazed at being alive.
Hard-working death goes frisking the age,
and everyone it finds turns that white.

The year looks around, lets out a scream,
looks around and falls into a swoon.
What an autumn lurks behind me again,
what a winter, numb with pain!

The woods bled; in revolving time
each single hour bled.
Enormous dark figures were
scribbled on snow by the wind.

I've lived to see this and that;
I feel a weight in the air;
a lukewarm silence full of tiny sounds
hugs me, as before my birth.

I pause here, at the base of the tree,
angrily it makes its crown creak.
A branch reaches down. To take me by the scruff?
I'm neither cowardly nor weak,

only tired. I keep still. And the branch too
musses my hair, scared and quiet.
One should forget, but I've never yet
forgotten a thing in all my life.

Clouds slide down on the moon; on the sky
poison draws a dark green stripe.
I roll myself a cigarette,
slowly, with care. I'm alive.

8 June 1940

52

IN MY MEMORIES ...

Flowers strolling in my memories ...
in a sudden shower I stand, at ease;
two women approach with wet, glistening teeth,
    then a pair of doves. Their round,
officious bellies reach all the way to the ground.

It's been a year. On the road to Senlis
mild, rainy dusk, and in some strange way
one moment brought me happiness again;
    green walls surrounded me,
quietly bowing, bending: it was a wood of ferns,

and from Ermenonville the youngish birch
grove ran to meet us like a simple-minded girl
wearing a white skirt, and at the bend
    a soldier stood in rows
of glinting highway mud. Between his teeth a rose.

It's as if light had swept across the sky. ...
Gyula sat facing me, and Zsuzsanna, shy,
beside me Fanni, in whose blue eyes passed
    the landscape, and not far
overhead flew the cheerful tassle of our car,

and dear, good Paris expected us by nightfall.
Swift death has rumbled past there something frightful
since then, and picked its colorful bouquet.
    Blushing, that birch grove still
wanders there among the warm and bloody swill,

and that brave tenant of the cold trenches grows,
supine, out of his heart, a shooting rose.
His country burns. Among the fires sway
    daydreaming cemeteries
fenced in by gnarled trees and walls perspiring away.

Above them burns a soot-filled, curling sky,
and yet, by evening, all the stars arrive,
and dawns weeping with dew are on the run
       toward the speechless sun.
I wonder, if I asked the land, would it reply?

In my memories strolling flowers ... .
I stand around in a passing shower;
down the road, a troop of women with children;
       sky smoke above their heads —
a cloud in shreds. Dissolving. Light and silver.

1940

SECOND ECLOGUE

Pilot:

Went far out in the night; I laughed, I was so mad.
Like swarms of bees the fighter planes buzzed overhead;
our defense was strong; friend! what a thick of firing,
until at last our new squadron showed on the horizon.
They all but picked me off and swept me up down there,
but look: I've returned. And come tomorrow, once more
cowardly Europe will creep to its air-raid hideaway. ...
Anyway — that'll do. Have you written since yesterday?

Poet:

I have; what else is there? Poets write; cats can say
meow; a dog must howl; the little fish will lay,
teasing, her roe of eggs. There's nothing I won't write of,
if only to let you know, up there, that I'm alive,
while between rows of houses exploding, walls caving in,
the light careens around, the blood-veined moon is swaying;
when, frightened out of sleep, the city's squares shall curl,
your breath is cut off, with nausea even the sky must whirl;
and the planes just keep coming: they disappear, and again,
like death-rattling insanity, one-and-all, swoop down!
I write: what else? And how filled a poem is with danger,
if you knew: how delicate a single line is, what a stranger
in its moods! this too takes courage. Poets write; cats
meow; a dog must howl; that little fish will let ...
and so on. And what's *your* lore? Nothing. You have an ear
for the engine, and your ear rings, now that you cannot hear;
don't even deny it: he's your friend, your siamese twin!
What's on your mind up there, when you're flying in the thin?

Pilot:

You'll laugh: I'm scared on those missions. I want my sweetheart;
I want to lie, down there, on a bed, my two eyes closed.
Or just to hum of her, strained softly between my teeth,
in that wild, steaming confusion, canteen-and-messhall-deep!
When I'm up, I want down; when down, I burn to fly;
there's no more room for me in this world, my kneaded dough.

55

And I know: my love for the plane has grown exaggerated,
true; but up there it's to one pulse the two of us must sting. ...
But you know and will write of it, a secret it will not stay:
I too lived like a man once, who now do nothing but destroy,
an outlaw of sky and earth. But who will understand it?
Will you write about me?

Poet:

If I live. And there's anyone around to read it.

27 April 1941

FRIDAY

April has gone insane,
the sun was taking its nap.
I drank for a solid week,
that's how I sobered up.

April has gone stark mad.
It whips you with frost and shiver;
someone writes and, weekly, sells
the country down the river.

April has gone insane.
There fell a crunching snow.
Many have taken flight,
their hearts have cracked in two.

April is raving mad:
it howls above the frost.
Three of my friends have left me;
all three of them are lost.

April is raving mad:
wild showers, erratic dose;
one of them lives; the fool has
no notion of what took place.

April has gone insane
and many rivers are flooded.
The second is no longer living,
two bullets lodge in his head.

It's been four days now: they killed him.
The third is a prisoner of war.
All our fruit crops freeze.
A smile around my mouth ...

You are to get even (I hear)
for everything. Take care!

18 May 1941

THIRD ECLOGUE

Pastoral Muse, be my company here, though I'm sitting inside: it's
only a sleepy café; light runs outdoors; in the pastures,
wordless, the mole digs deep; earth grows little humps, turns humpback;
and fine-bodied, white-toothed, brown-skinned fishermen sleep on
slippery bottoms of fish boats, after the labors of daybreak.

Pastoral Muse, stay with me here, too, in the copse of downtown, where
salesmen, these seven, make noise; but don't let the seven here scare you
off; believe me, right now plenty worries their minds, poor old fellows! ...
then look at *them* on your right — all jurists! and none of them plays his
flute any more, to be sure, but my, how they blow that cigar smoke!

Come, sit with me! I teach, and between two lessons I've dropped in,
trying to think, on the wings of smoke, about love and its wonders.
Just as a cockeyed, droplet bird whistle shall resurrect that
dried-out tree, so I thought it had lifted me bright, had flown me
onto the young-old rooftops, to teen-age wilds of desire.

Shepherdess Muse, be my ally! the horns of dawn blare music
only of her! their vaporfilled voices now sing of her body,
all her glowing form; of the slim, bright smile of her eyelids;
sighs: how they come on her lips with carefully tutored dance steps;
sing of her movement, embrace, her admiring the moon in the heavens!

Pastoral Muse, give advice! let me celebrate love in my poems;
sorrow is clawing me deep, new pain on the heels of the world now,
ever and nothing but new! like others, I too will soon perish.
Trees grow crooked and gnarled, and the mouths of salt mines cave in;
bricks must scream in a wall — so I dream it, at least, when I'm sleeping.

Pastoral Muse, be my guide! in this age it is poets who die like ...
heaven will topple on us, no grave mound marks our dust here,
nor will a nobly conceived Greek amphora hold them; if one, two
poems of ours remain ... may I write about love, just a line more?
Look how her body sends light — o Shepherdess Muse, be my tutor!

12 June 1941

58

SIMILES

You're like a whispering branch
when leaning over me,
you're just like poppy seed,
your flavor a mystery,

like time unceasingly growing its rings,
you're that exciting,
and again as calming
as a gravestone marking a grave,

you're a friend who grew up with me, tall and fair,
and even now
I don't quite know
the perfume of your heavy hair,

then you're blue, and I worry: you may leave me;
you're roving, slender smoke,
I'm afraid of you as you take
on the color of lightning,

like a sunlit, celestial war
in darker gold —
o when you hold
anger you're like the deep-voiced, clear

vowel *ú* — long-resonant and dark,
and at times like these
I draw around you
out of a smile a shining arc.

16 November 1941

SPRING IS IN FLIGHT ...

Preface to the Eclogues

Ice on the river is sliding, the riverbank spots up in darkness;
snow is melting; already a babyfaced sunray bathes in
infant puddles left by the footprints of deer and of rabbits.
Spring is in flight, her hair disheveled, past lounging mountains,
down in the depths of mine shafts, holes that the burrowing moles made,
runs along tree roots, in buds: at the base of their sensitive armpits,
rests on the stems of ticklish leaves, before hurrying onward.
And on the meadows all over, on hillcrests, on lakesurf, the skyvault
    bursts into summerblue flame.

Spring is in flight, with her hair undone, but the angel of ancient
freedom lies by her side no longer; he sleeps, deep-frozen
yellow, in mud, as he lies among comatose roots; he is sleep-drugged,
cannot see light down there, nor perceive on the tree brush hosts of
curling, small green leaves; it cannot be helped! he won't waken.
Prisoner. Into his dreams there splashes a jailed man's bewildered,
ring-shaping sorrow, while earth and frozen night weigh his heart down.
Dreamer; and even his sighs won't lift his silent breast now,
    no ice cracks in those depths.

Deafmute root: sound off! speak, leaves with your knife-sharp voices!
sing it out, dog with the foaming mouth! fish: splash on that water!
Shake away at that mane, horse! bellow, bull! streambed, let's hear you!
    Sleeper, awake from your sleep!

11 April 1942

SUDDENLY

Suddenly one night the wall moves,
silence trumpets into the heart and a groan flies out.
Pain knifes the ribs, behind them even a heartbeat
    used to trouble, goes mute.
Only the wall cries out; the body lifts, dumb and deaf.
And the heart, the hand, and the mouth know, here, this is death,
    it is death.

As when in prison electricity winks,
the inmates inside and the guard walking his clinks
know how in one body all current runs together;
mum's the word for a bulb, a shadow runs through a cell,
and now the guards, the inmates, the worms know it's burned
    human flesh they smell.

20 April 1942

NIGHT

Hearts are asleep, in hearts apprehension is sleeping, and fear,
flies are asleep on the wall with a cobweb, amazing how near;
silence indoors, not a scratch from the vigilant mouse,
garden and branch are asleep, and the snipe in its house;
bee in the beehive asleep, and the fly in the rose,
sleeping in kernels of wheat all the summer wheat knows;
flame in the moon sleeps cold, a medallion of light;
autumn arises to steal: now it steals in the night.

1 June 1942

END-OF-OCTOBER HEXAMETERS

White-laughing brook, in its dance-stepping bed, runs down from the mountains;
dancing, an autumn leaf smooths flat on its crest as it floats past.
Look how the dogwood flashes its tart-flavored jewels in shadow;
minuscule grass blades flash in the sunlight, old in their trembling.
Sun still shines, but it's so ripe that only a leisurely reason
holds it aloft to prevent its fall: it fears for its massed gold.
Slow I am, bright myself in this slow and intelligent brightness.
I too fear for you in the winter cold; blind worries:
thoughts of firewood, winter clothes, grow large in your eyes, then
wane as, with breath, their mirrors befog. Then somnolent sorrow
wells in the brilliant blue; what you speak falls asleep on your lips, and
kisses awaken. The snow comes black, and winter does likewise;
corners of huge fall sky are already abloom with the blackness;
hours of dawn take slippery steps. Come to sleep, under trailing
beards of evenings; and look: I'm your child, but also your grownup
son, come of age, and your lover, ripe for the half of our hardships,
serious, not only for verse. We'll lie and I'll listen with night-tuned
ears to the pulse of anxiety asleep on your heart in the darkness.
So I will listen and wait. And just as a fledgling stork, come
autumn, learning to fly, will stumble and halt on the sky's waves,
so I will toss on our spacious bed, fly slowly on, sighing.
Taking the sighs on myself, I'll know their rhythmic beat will
lull us to sleep, in our single care. And as dreams take us captive,
hear in the night how autumn's wet flag slaps at the dark air.

Élesd-Nagytelekmajor,
28 September — 14 November 1942

63

WINTER SUNSHINE

The molten snow caves in
and prowls about as it goes;
kettles stand about, steaming
like purple, baked sweet potatoes.

An icicle keeps on stretching,
its waterdrop gaining in weight;
here, there a puddle goes popping
with a gentle skyward gaze.

And up on the shelf of the sky
the snow has been sliding back;
I've become a man of few words,
my arguing voice has grown weak.

And: waiting around for a meal,
am I, or about to die?
Will I make a fluttering soul,
bruising both night and day?

My shadow glances at me,
while the winter sun is overcast.
I'm wearing a treasury cap,
and the sun is sporting a hat.

26 December 1942

FOURTH ECLOGUE

Poet:
If you had only asked me in my seedling age ...
O yes, I knew, I knew!
I don't want the world! It's rude! I shouted in rage.
Dull darkness slams me, and the light cuts me through!
And I survived. My head has long since healed.
And my lungs only grew stronger for all those times I howled.

Voice;
And the red waves of scarlet fever
and of measles all cast you ashore.
Once it wanted to swallow you — then the lake spat you out.
Why do you think time took you up in her arms after all?
And the heart, the liver, the two wing-shaped lungs,
the waterlogged, mysterious machine,
that it should serve you — to what end? And the horrible flower
cancer is not yet blossoming in your flesh.

Poet:
I was born. I protested. And yet I am here.
I am grown. You ask me, To what end? I just don't know.
Always I would have wanted to be free,
and guards escorted me down the avenue.

Voice:
You've walked on mountain peaks bright with wind,
and seen, as evening came, among the hill's
stunted bushes a gentle roebuck kneeling;
seen, on treetrunks standing in sunlight, drops of resin,
and a naked young woman step from the river,
and once a great stag-beetle alighted on your hand. ...

Poet:
I can't even see this much from captivity.
Had I only been born a mountain, a plant, or a bird ... ,
just a consoling thought fluttering past,
an empty boast. Help me, liberty,
let me find my true home at last.

That peak again, the woods, the woman, the bushes,
the soul's wings burning in the wind!
And help me be reborn into a new world,
when from among golden vapors the sun's
light blinds and rises on ever-fresh dawns.

It's still quiet, quiet, but the storm now breathes;
ripe fruits hang on the branches.
A butterfly is swept on light breezes, it flies.
Death already whistles among the trees.

And now I know: I too will ripen to death,
surfing time bore me up, will drop me again;
I have served time, and slowly my solitude
grows as does the crest of the crescent moon.

I shall be free, earth will dissolve me,
and up above the ground a broken world
stands in slow flames. The writing tablets are cracked.
Fly up, imagination, on your heavy wings!

Voice:
The fruit swings and will fall, once it is ripe;
earth, deep with memory, will lay you to rest.
But for now, let your anger's smoke rise to the sky,
and write on the sky when all below lies wrecked!

15 March 1943

HESITANT ODE

How long I've been rehearsing to tell you
of the hidden constellation of my love,
but perhaps only in images, and the essence alone.
Still, in me you're tumult, and flooding, like life,
and at times you're as secure and as eternal
as a fossilized snail shell in a stone.
High overhead moves a night streaked with the moon
and hunts down buzzing-starting, flying little dreams.
And I still can't tell you of the full extent
of what it means to me, while I'm working,
to feel your protective gaze over my hand.
Similes don't do much. They emerge; I discard them.
And, come morning, I'll start it all over again,
for I'm worth no more than the value of the word
in my poem, and because this will have me worried
until nothing is left of me but tufts of hair and bones.
You're tired; I myself feel it's been a long day —
what more should I say? Objects exchange glances,
and they praise you: half a sugar cube sings
on the table top, and a drop of honey falls
and shines on the cloth, a sphere of pure gold,
and, all by itself, an empty water glass rings out.
He's happy he lives with you. And how he waits for your steps —
perhaps I'll have time yet, and all this can be told.
Off and on I'm touched by the falling dusk of dreams:
it flies away, then returns to rest on your brow;
your sleepy eyes say goodbye, an acknowledging nod;
your hair comes undone, it spreads out and streams,
and you sleep. The long shadow of your eyelashes has moved.
Your hand falls on my pillow: a birch twig gone to sleep,
but I too sleep within you: you're not *another* world.
And I hear all the way how the multitude
of mysterious, thin, and sage lines keep changing
                                    in the cool palm of your hand.

26 May 1943

COLUMBUS

"In Nomine Domini Nostri Jhesu Christi" —
That's how he once began. No time now for his diary.
Wind turns the pages. He leaves it, has other thoughts;
above him there purrs a wild, taut sky with giant claws.

Columbus, legs apart, stands firm, and in the night
four mutineers sit crouched in bases of the masts;
the great ship pitches, rolls; the many sails hum a note.

Could Rodrigo be wrong? Perhaps. ... Frog in his throat.
But don't the tufts of grass point to approaching land?
and I saw them myself: fly, flock of birds, fly west,
and yesterday, a dove.

                And "Land! Land!" howls the crow's nest.
And it was on a Friday, at 2 a.m., and at dark dawn.
"Laudetur" — they murmured and stood, hats in hand.

1 June 1943

THE TERRIBLE ANGEL

Today the terrible angel is invisible,
silent within me; he does not howl.
But you hear a muffled sound, perk up,
it's no more than if you heard a grasshopper pop,
looked around, and hadn't any notion who it was.
He is the one. Cautious today. Makes ready.
Defend me with your love. Love me heroically.
He cowers when you're with me, turns courageous
as soon as you're gone. He breaks from the dregs
of the soul and, screaming, wildly accuses.
Insanity. He works in me like poison,
and sleeps but seldom. He lives inside,
and outside me as well. On white,
moonlit nights he runs in sandals that, rustling, move
over fields, and rummages, also in my mother's grave.
"Was it worth it?" he asks her every time,
awakening her. He whispers to her, inciting,
choking: "You gave him birth and died of it!"
Now and then he glances at me, tears off, ahead
of time, the calendar's pages that wait their turn.
Already, for me, the final word
on: "How long?" "Where to?" is his. His tone
fell into my heart last night, as a stone
falls into water, sending out
circles that floated and whirred.
Quietly I was just getting ready;
you were asleep by then. I stood
naked when he came to me in the night
and, half in silence, started an argument.
Some strange odor flew by, and a freezing
breath struck my ear: "Continue undressing!"
he cheered me on. "Not even skin should hide you bare.
Raw meat and exposed nerve is all you are!

Go on: flay yourself. None but a fool
would boast of his skin as of his very own jail.
It's only a mask on you; come: here's the knife;
it won't hurt; it's but a split-second, a hiss stifled!"

And on the table lay the awakening, gleaming knife.

4 August 1943

PARIS

At the corner of Boulevard St. Michel
and Rue Cujas the sidewalk slants a bit.
I have not abandoned you, beautiful,
wild weeks of youth — your voice, like an echoing
mine shaft, still reverberates in my heart.
Corner Rue M. le Prince: that's where the baker lived.

And from the left, from among the park's great trees,
one flamed so brightly yellow against the sky,
it must have foreseen that fall was on its way.
Freedom, nymph whom I love, long of thigh,
dressed in the twilight's golden rays,
do you still play hide-and-seek among the veillike trees?

Summer came through like a movement of troops,
raised dust on the road and perspired, drumming;
close on his heels flew some cooling vapors,
on both sides you could feel the fragrance spreading.
Noon was still summer; that afternoon, in tow,
sweet autumn came, our guest, dripping with rainy brow.

Back then I lived just like a child:
as I wished; then too like a pedantic old
man who now knows: the earth is round.
I was still green; my beard suggested snow.
I took walks, and who gave it another thought?
Later on I descended to the torrid underworld.

Where are you, sudden music of subway stops:
CHÂTELET – CITÉ – St. MICHEL – ODÉON!
and: DENFERT-ROCHEREAU – you sound like a curse.
Large, stained wall: flowerlike, a map would blow.
Where are you? Ho! — I shout. I listen.
Body odor and ozone start in together, hissing.

Not to speak of the nights! the pilgrim path
of midnight: outskirts to the Quartier.
Will the dawn over Paris, strangely wrath-
filled, overcast, light up once more in gray,
when, home from writing verse, drunk in the head,
already half asleep, I undress to go to bed?

And will I have the strength left to return
from heavy cross-currents of my waning life?
The cat from the cheap, fetid restaurant
downstairs, was mating up on our roof.
Oh, how he whined! Will I ever hear him again?
That's when I learned in what incessant din
Noah must have floated under his ancient moon.

14 August 1943

FIFTH ECLOGUE

To the memory of György Bálint

Fragment

Dear Friend, if you but knew how I've shivered with cold from this poem,
standing in fear of the word, so that even today I have fled it.
Hemistichs: all I could write.
                            I tried making *others* my subject,
tried, and in vain! for the night, this terrible, secretive evening,
calls on me: write about *him*.
                            And I start from my sleep, but the voice is
silent, as are those dead on the fields — the Ukraine — all silent.
Missing.
            And this fall didn't bring word of you, either.
                                                        In forests,
today, winter's feral prophecies whisper, and weighted
clouds pull on and, filled with snow, stop again on the skyways.
Are you alive? who would know?
                            I don't myself any more; have
stopped getting angry when, waving, they painfully cover their faces,
knowing nothing.
                But *are* you still living? or were you just wounded?
Do you take walks in the leaves, in the forest muck's thick perfume, or
are you a fragrance yourself?
                            On the meadows the snowflakes are flying.
Missing — slam: goes the news.
                            And the heart beats within, then freezes.
In between my ribs there awakens a tense, bad feeling,
trembling pain now, and in my memories words you once left us
live with an edge so sharp, and I feel your reality, body,
as of the dead —
                And despite this, I cannot write about you this evening!

21 November 1943

I CANNOT KNOW ...

I cannot know what these parts could mean to someone else;
to me it's home, this tiny land in the embrace
of flames, since childhood cradling from far-off, my world.
It's out of her I grew, as does from a trunk its tender shoot,
and I hope that one day my body will sink into this soil.
I am at home. And when a bush kneels, once in a while,
at my feet, I know its name and can name its blossom;
I know where people are headed on the road, as I know them;
and know what, in the summer sunset, it could mean
when from the tenement walls there trickles a reddish pain.
Take a man in a plane: to him it's a map, this country;
he could not point to the home of Mihály Vörösmarty —
what do maps hold for him? Wild army posts, factories,
for me: grasshoppers, oxen, towers, farms, gentle fields;
he sees factories, corn fields through his binoculars,
while I also see concerned, apprehensive laborers,
forests, resplendent orchards, vineyards, and cemeteries,
among the gravestones a granny who softly weeps and weeps,
and what from high up are rail lines to be destroyed, or plants,
are here a signal tower, before which a lineman stands,
signals, red flag in hand, with many children around,
and in the plant yard, a shepherd dog rolling on the ground.
And there is the park, with footsteps of old lovers still there,
sweet kisses in my mouth, cranberry-, honey-clear;
and, going to school, on the sidewalk's edge along the way,
I stepped on a stone, sure thing, so as not to recite that day —
here: see this stone, from up there? Try as you might, you can't;
to show all this in fine detail — there is no such instrument.

We are guilty without a doubt, as are other nations too;
we know how we have transgressed, when, where, and in what way;
but there do live workers here, and poets too, innocent,
and suckling infants in whom there grows intelligence;
it glows in them, they guard it, hidden away in dark cellars
until peace should once again mark this land with its finger,
and they will answer our choked words in phrasing clear and loud.

Spread over us your great wing, vigil nocturnal cloud.

17 January 1944

IN A CLAMOROUS PALM TREE

In a clamorous palm tree
I'd like to sit most of all,
in a shivering earthly body
a crouching skyborn soul.

Up in that tree I'd sit
with a circle of learned apes,
their cutting voices would rain on me
brilliant as hail;

I'd study their melodies,
and would sing with the crew,
cheerfully lost in wonder
at how their noses and rumps are
a uniform blue.

An enormous sun would burn
above the dwelled-in trees,
and I'd burn with shame
for all humanity;

the apes would understand me,
their minds are still in good health.
Perhaps if I lived among them,
I too would attain to that mercy —
a kindly death.

5 April 1944

THE EXILE

From the window I look out on a hill,
    the hill does not see me;
I hide out; a poem trickles from my pen,
    though it makes no difference now.
I see it, unable to figure out why
    such grace from an ancient bosom:
as ever, the moon alights on the sky,
    and the sour cherries open into blossom.

9 May 1944

MAY PICNIC

Victrola sits resounding in the grass,
like one pursued it's out of breath, it groans.
But instead of pursuers it's girls
who surround it, like fiery flowers.

A little girl kneels down, turns over a side,
her back is brown, her legs are still white;
on the bad music her child-soul lifts away,
and, like the clouds up there, it's perfectly gray.

Boys are crouching, and they burn like embers,
with words on their lips, both clumsy and tender;
their bodies are tense with tiny victories,
and when they'll have to kill, they'll do it at ease.

Perhaps they could still turn into humankind,
for, after all, that portion of the mind
worthy of men is in them, only asleep.
O tell me that it's not without some hope.

10 May 1944

DREAM LANDSCAPE

To the memory of Clemens Brentano

When the lampblack of night comes dropping,
when the mood of the sky at dusk wilts down,
then night overhead in the waterdeep silence
will weave at its star-woven crown.

When the head of the moon in the sky is bleeding,
and the light in the lake cuts circling rills,
over the yellow countryside shadows come stealing
and climb up the rims of the hills.

And while under the nests with starting-up hearts
beating loud, they prepare in the woods for the dance,
the fish splashing down on the mirror are watched
by drifting leaves with their somnolent glance.

Then all of a sudden the land of my dream
flaps its great wings, swims on in the clear;
on the cloudbedded sky there drifts a bird,
afraid, driven on by its fear,

and solitude in my heart is tamer
and the thought of dying, nearer.

27 October 1943 — 16 May 1944

SEVENTH ECLOGUE

Look how evening descends and around us the barbed-wire-hemmed, wild
oaken fence and the barracks are weightless, as evening absorbs them.
Slowly your glance lets go of the frame of our captive condition,
only the mind, it alone is alive to the tautness of wire.
See, Love: fantasy has one way to attain to its freedom,
namely, through dream, that comely redeemer who liberates broken
bodies — it's time, and the men in the camp all leave for their homes now.

Ragged, with shaven heads, these prisoners, snoring aloud, fly
leaving Serbia's blind peak, back to their fugitive homesteads.
Fugitive homesteads — right. ... Dear one, is our house still standing?
still untouched by bombs? as it stood, back when we reported?
And will the men who now groan on my right, lie left, make it home yet?
Is there a home, where people can savor hexameter language?

No diacritics. Just one line under another line: groping,
barely, as I am alive, I write my poem in half-dark,
blindly, in earthworm-rhythm, I'm inching along on the paper.
Flashlights, books: the guards of the *Lager* took everything from us,
nor does the mail ever come. Only fog settles over the barracks.

Here among rumors and worms all live, be they Frenchmen or Polish,
loud-voiced Italian, partisan Serb, sad Jew, in the mountains,
bodies hacked and in fever; yet all live a life held in common:
waiting for good news, a loving, womanly word, for a fate free,
human; awaiting the end, plumbing dusk, or a miracle — maybe.

Worm-riddled, captive beast: that is just how I lie on the plank boards.
Fleas will renew their siege; the batallion of flies is asleep now.
Evening is here; once again our serfdom has grown a day shorter,
so have our lives. The camp is asleep. On mountain and valley
bright moon shines; in its light once more all the wires pull tighter,
and through the window you see how the shadows of camp's armed, pacing
sentries are thrown on the wall in the midst of the night's lone voices.

Camp is asleep, dear one: can you see us? The dreams come rustling;
starting, one will snort on his narrow bunk, turn over;
sleeping again, his face shines. Lonely the vigil I'm keeping;
in my mouth I taste that half-smoked cigarette, not your
kisses, and dreams won't come, no sleep will come to relieve me,
since I can face neither death nor a life any longer without you.

Lager Heidenau, above Žagubica in the mountains,
July 1944

LETTER TO MY WIFE

Down in the deep, dumb worlds are waiting, silent;
I shout; the silence in my ears is strident,
but no one can send it reply from far
Serbia, fallen into a swoon of war,
and you are far. Your voice braids my dream;
by day I find it in my heart again;
knowing this I keep still, while, standing proudly,
rustling, cool to the touch, many great ferns surround me.

When might I see you? I hardly know any longer,
you, who were solid, were weighty as the psalter,
beautiful as a shadow and beautiful as light,
to whom I would find my way, whether deafmute or blind;
now hiding in the landscape, from within
my eyes, you flash — the mind projects its film.
You were what is real, returned to dream in essence,
and I, relapsed into the well of adolescence,

jealously question you: whether you love me,
whether, on my youth's summit, you will yet be
my wife — I am now hoping once again,
and, back on life's alert road, where I have fallen,
I know you are all this. My wife, my friend and peer —
only, far! Beyond three wild frontiers.
It is turning fall. Will fall forget me here?
The memory of our kisses is all the clearer.

I had faith in miracles, forgot their days;
above me I see a bomber squadron cruise.
I was just admiring, up there, your eyes' blue sheen,
when it clouded over, and up in that machine
the bombs were aching to dive. Despite them, I am alive,
a prisoner; and all I had hoped for, I have
sized up, in breadth. I will find my way to you;
for you I have walked the spirit's full length as it grew,

and highways of the land. If need be, I will render
myself, a conjurer, past cardinal embers,
amid nose-diving flames, but I will come back,
if I must be, I shall be resilient as the bark
on trees. I am soothed by the peace of savage men
living in trouble: worth the whole wild regimen
of arms and power; and, as from a cooling wave of the sea,
the light of *2 x 2* is raining down on me.

Lager Heidenau, above Žagubica in the mountains,
August-September 1944

ROOT

Power flashes in a root;
it drinks rain, lives down below,
and its dreams are white as snow.

From under earth it breaks upward;
it climbs, and is sly, that root,
has an arm just like a rope.

On a root's arm, a worm asleep;
a worm sits on a root's leg;
with worms the whole world is plagued.

But in the deep the root lives on.
It cares not a hang for the world,
only for a branch that leaves have filled.

This it admires and nurses,
sends it excellent flavors,
good sweet sky-ripened flavors.

I am now a root myself —
it's with worms I make my home,
there, I am completing this poem.

Once a flower, I have turned root,
heavy, dark earth over hand and foot;
fate fulfilled, and all is said,
a saw now wails above my head.

Lager Heidenau, above Žagubica in the mountains,
8 August 1944

À LA RECHERCHE ...

Evenings, gentle and old, you return as memory's nobles!
Gleaming table, crowned, as by laurels, with poets and young wives,
where are you sliding on marshes of irretrievable hours?
Where are the nights when exuberant friends were cheerfully drinking
auvergnat gris out of brown-eyed, thin-stemmed, delicate glasses?

Lines of verse swam high round the light of the lamps, with bright green
features bobbing up-down foaming crests of the meter;
those now dead were alive and the prisoners, still at home; those
vanished, dear friends, long since fallen, were writing their poems;
on their hearts the Ukraine, the soil of Spain or of Flanders.

There were those who, gritting their teeth, ran ahead in the fire,
combat-trained, and only because they were helpless against it,
and while the company slept its troubled sleep in its soiled
shelter of night, their rooms made the rounds of their wakeful dreaming,
rooms that in this society had served them as island and cavern.

Places there were where some went in sealed-off cattle cars; places
where they, stiff with fear and unarmed, stood erect in the minefields;
places where, rifle in hand, not a few of them went of their own will,
silent, because they felt that war, down there, was their own cause —
Angel of Freedom, you'll guard their enormous dreams in the night now.

Places too ... never mind. What with sage wine nights disappearing ...
Flying, the callups came round; the poems left scraps grew in numbers,
as did wrinkles swarm at corners of mouths, under eyes: young
women's once-beautiful smiles; and the girls with the fairy-tale-princess
steps: how heavy they grew in the course of the taciturn war years!

Where are the nights and the tavern, the table set out under lindens?
those still alive, whom war's heel flat-ground for nothing but combat?
This heart hears their voices; my hand holds the warmth of their handshakes.
Quoting their work, I watch the proportions of torsos unfold; I
measure them (prisoner, mute) — sigh-filled, up in Serbia's mountains.

Where, where indeed is the night? that night which shall never return now,
for, to whatever is past, death itself lends another perspective.
Here at the table they sit, take shelter in smiles of the women,
and will yet take sips from our glasses, those many unburied
sleeping in forests of foreign, on meadows of faraway places.

Lager Heidenau, above Žagubica in the mountains,
17 August 1944

EIGHTH ECLOGUE

Poet:
Greetings! you're keeping in fine form, walking the mountain's wild trail,
handsome old man; is it wings bear you high or do enemies give chase?
Wings lift, emotions pursue you, and lightning flashes from both eyes.
Welcome up, wizened Sir; I can see you are one of those ancient
prophets, of mountainous wrath, but which of that school, can you tell me?

Prophet:
Which, you say? Náhum's my name, and Elkósh is the city that bore me;
ringing I railed against Nineveh, lustful Assyrian city,
singing the word of God: I was known as the stuffed bag of anger!

Poet:
Ancient ire; I know it: your words have survived, and we have them.

Prophet:
Yes, they've survived. But abundant vice is around, more than ever,
and the design of the Lord is a mystery now, as it was then.
Some things the Lord did say: that the richest of rivers would run dry;
that Mt. Carmel would fall; that the flower of Lebanon, Báshan
was to wither; that mountains would shake and that fire would consume all.
All came to pass.

Poet:
                Swift nations are busily killing one another;
as at Nineveh, here it's the spirit of man running naked.
What are all speeches worth; what good are the hog-pestilential
green clouds — locusts — now? Of all beasts, aren't humans the lowest?
Here as there, they'll splatter the infants' heads on the ramparts;
belfries are torches; apartment buildings are ovens; the tenants
bake inside; and factories fly into air in a smoke cloud.
Streets run amok with burning citizens, faint with the sirens;
bomb craters boil over as, heavily, payloads nose-dive;
and as on pastures cow pies, so on the squares of the city,
shrunken the dead lie about; once again all the grief you predicted
happened just as you wrote that it would. And despite that, what brought you
back to this earth from the ancient funnel cloud?

Prophet:

Rage did. That men stand
orphaned again — have stood since! — in armies of man-shaped pagans.
And, once again, I'd like nothing more than to witness the guilty
citadels' fall, then to speak to a subsequent age as a witness.

Poet:

That you have done. And God did, long ago, say through your own words:
Fortresses filled with prey, where they pull up that battlement, using
corpses as building stone: watch out! but tell me: could anger
stoke you for thousands of years, with such heavenly, obstinate fire?

Prophet:

Ages ago, once, the Lord touched *my* distorted mouth too,
as he did wise Isaiah's with coals, with his red-glowing embers,
making my heart confess, and the coals were alive, incandescent
— it was an angel who held them with tongs — and: "Here I am, take me,
call on me too to be preaching your word!" I said, as he vanished.
And whom the Lord has once sent out — that man, become ageless,
lives without sleep. What burns his lips are those coals of the angel.
What, after all, are a thousand years to the Lord? Time is feathers!

Poet:

Yes, you are young, my father! I envy you. Dare I compare my
vanishing days with your awesome age? Yet, just as a wild brook
wears down a pebble, this fugitive moment is wearing me flat, smooth.

Prophet:

So you believe. I know your new work. Fury sustains you.
Anger of prophets, of poets: they're closely related, and nations
find them their food and drink. Those who'll live, could live on it till that
kingdom arrived which a certain youthful disciple had promised:
rabbi, who came and fulfilled our law and the word of the prophets.
Come, proclaim with me that the hour is close, very close — that
kingdom is being born now. What is God's plan and what is his purpose?
I once asked, and see: it's that kingdom. We'll take to the road. Let's
gather the tribe, bring your wife, and start cutting sticks for the journey.
Wanderers find companionship in a walking stick; look,
do let that one there be mine: I prefer having one with deep knots.

Lager Heidenau, above Žagubica in the mountains,
23 August 1944

FORCED MARCH

The man who, having collapsed,   rises, takes steps, is insane;
he'll move an ankle, a knee,   a pilgrim to his pain,
and take to the road again   as if wings were to lift him high;
the ditch calls him in vain: he simply dare not stay;
and should you ask, why not?   perhaps he'll turn and answer:
his wife is waiting back home,   and a death, one beautiful, wiser.
A cinch: the wretch is a fool,   for over the homes, that world,
long since nothing but singed   winds have been known to whirl;
his house wall lies supine;   your plum tree, broken clear,
and all the nights back home   horripilate with fear.
Oh, if I could believe   that I haven't merely saved
what is worthwhile, in my heart;   that home can still receive;
tell me it's all still there: the cool verandah, bees
buzzing in peaceful silence   (while the plum jam cools!);
end-of-the-summer quiet,   sunbathing, sleepy, bent
over gardens: leaves and fruit,   naked and redolent;
that, blonde, my Fanni is waiting   before the redwood fence,
where morning slowly traces   its shadowed reticence. ...
But all that *could* return —   just look at tonight's full moon!
Don't go past me, my friend —   shout! and I'll rise again.

Bor, 15 September 1944

PICTURE POSTCARDS

(1)

From Bulgaria thick, wild cannon pounding rolls.
It strikes the mountain ridge, then hesitates and falls.
A traffic jam of thoughts, animals, carts, and men;
whinnying the road rears up; the sky runs with its mane.
In this chaos of movement you're in me, permanent,
deep in my conscious you shine, motion forever spent
and mute, like an angel awed by death's great carnival,
or an insect in rotted tree pith, staging its funeral.

30 August 1944. In the mountains.

(2)

Nine kilometers from here the haystacks and
houses are burning;
sitting on the fields' edges, some scared and speechless
poor folk are smoking.
Here a little shepherdess, stepping onto the lake,
ruffles the water;
the ruffled sheep flock at the water drinks from
clouds, bending over.

Cservenka, 6 October 1944

(3)

Bloody saliva hangs on the mouths of the oxen.
Blood shows in every man's urine.
The company stands in wild knots, stinking.
Death blows overhead, revolting.

Mohács, 24 October 1944

(4)

I fell beside him; his body turned over,
already taut as a string about to snap.
Shot in the back of the neck. That's how you too will end,
I whispered to myself: just lie quietly.
Patience now flowers into death.
Der springt noch auf, a voice said above me.
On my ear, blood dried, mixed with filth.

Szentkirályszabadja, 31 October 1944

Page 29, "Sunbodied Virgins, Shepherds and Flocks":
Some of the imagery of this poem may well form a partial background of the later impulse to cultivate the eclogue form. The threatened idyllic setting is certainly perceivable already in this early piece.

Page 31, "C. Neumann & Söhne":
The title of the poem derives without a doubt from the name of the textile manufacturing plant at Liberec where Radnóti had his on-the-job training in 1927-1928. The "Reichenberg" poetry also includes part of a landscape cycle of six poems, a "Nocturno," and a fourteen-poem "Love Cycle from 1927-28." The careful dating of the poems (a feature they share with all of the published poetry) shows that Radnóti was back in Budapest by the early days of July 1928.

Page 35, "8 December 1931":
The "Dr. Kornél Melléky" of the dedication is, to all appearances, his defense attorney at the trial the poem commemorates.

Line 20 "two of my poems": for a facsimile of one of them, "Fall Berries Ripen in the Sun Now," see Baróti, p. 80.

Page 37, "While Writing":
Line 12 refers without a doubt to Kazinczy's later career, following his seven-year imprisonment (1794-1801) for his implication in the Jacobin Martinovics conspiracy. After his release Kazinczy married and retired from public life, to his estate at Széphalom. A parallel more familiar to English-speaking readers (without the imprisonment) might be Milton after the Restoration.

Pages 40-41, "Cartes Postales":
For a brief comparison of this cycle with the ultimate "Picture Postcards" see Ortutay, *Kortárs* 3:652 (also in Baróti, p. 7).

No attempt has been made to reproduce the rhymes in "Jardin du Luxembourg" or in "Quai de Montebello."

Page 42, "Song about Death":
Kosztolányi was as fine a novelist and short story writer as he was a poet. Deeply conscious socially, he probably influenced Radnóti as much as Margit Kaffka did. The poem suggests that the two men were personally acquainted. Kosztolányi's work has been translated in this country; see, for example, his novella "The Train-Robber," translated by Agnes H. Allison, *Accent* 10 (Autumn 1950): 213-18.

The imagery in stanza 3 is well worth comparing with that of the Bor poem "Root."

Page 45, "Go to Sleep":
Line 6 "Guernica": The events of the Spanish Civil War, with which Radnóti first became acquainted on his second trip to Paris in 1937, are mourned by the poet in a number of his works; see, besides this poem, "Marginal Note to the Prophet Habakkuk," "First Eclogue," "Hispania, Hispania," "Federico García Lorca," "Thursday," and "À la recherche ... ." Cf. Baróti, pp. 122-29.

Page 46, "Il faut laisser":
Line 1, quotation: Ronsard's choice, as well as Radnóti's, may well have been motivated by Horace's "linquenda tellus et domus et placens / uxor" ("we must leave earth, and home, and sweet wife") *(Odes* 2.14.21-22).

Line 2 "one of his last poems": the work alluded to is number 6 of a closing six-sonnet cycle in Ronsard's posthumously published *Les Derniers Vers* (1586). See *Les Oeuvres de Pierre de Ronsard, Texte de 1587,* ed. Isidore Silver, 8 (Chicago, 1970): 107; a literal English translation will be found in K. R. W. Jones, *Pierre de Ronsard* (New York, 1970), p. 144.

Line 16 "Just wait": although the context here is univocal, and the theme of death is underscored by the mood of the poem, the language of the concluding line strongly brings to mind the last two lines of Goethe's famous nine-line poem, "Über allen Gipfeln" ("Over All Mountaintops"): "Just wait, soon / You too will rest." Goethe's influence may also be felt in poems that work with images of wandering or of the moon (e.g. "Sky with Clouds").

Pages 47-48, "First Eclogue":
The epigraph is from Vergil *Georgics* 1.505-506; translation: "For here are right and wrong inverted; so many wars overrun the world, so many are the shapes of sin" *(Virgil,* trans. H. Rushton Fairclough, Loeb Classical Library [London, 1930], 1:115).

Lines 16-18: by the time of his death Lorca's reputation was as firmly established in Europe as it was in the Western Hemisphere. Since the early, and very positive, study by Edwin Honig in New Directions' "The Makers of Modern Literature" series (Norfolk, Conn., 1944), Lorca's reputation seems to have suffered somewhat, at least in the scholarship, for in a relatively recent handbook we read: "... in Spain an early inflation of achievement has been followed recently by a general denigration. He was not a major poet and some of his work now appears rather tawdry" *(The Concise Encyclopedia of Modern World Literature,* ed. Geoffrey Grigson [New York, 1963], s.v. García Lorca).

Line 25 "Attila József didn't escape": József committed suicide in 1937 by jumping in front of a freight train. See the facsimile of Radnóti's diary entry on the occasion of József's death in Baróti, p. 148; there, among other observations, Radnóti writes: "He lived in humiliating poverty, among constant and ever more frequent political disappointments. Only one other poet in Hungarian literature died so *natural* a death, Sándor Petőfi, ..." The implied triad "Petőfi–József–Radnóti" seems inescapable at such a moment as this (see also the Introduction to this volume).

Page 49, "In a Restless Hour":
It is rather likely that by January 1939 Radnóti had read not only the odes of Horace, but also those of Hölderlin. The influence of the German poet, especially of such a subjectively attuned mature poem in Alcaics as "Die Heimat" ("Home"), on Radnóti's sole Alcaic ode, seems unmistakable. The mention of Empedocles in the "Palinode" section of the poem "Perhaps ..." (July 1940) also has a Hölderlinian ring.

Page 50, "Thursday":
This poem contains more on faraway events, although it is more than likely that the initials in lines 2, 5, and 7 are personae of Hungarians who went abroad and found their lots unhappy. The mixture, in the entire poem, of the styles of four such different poets as Petőfi, Ady, Heine, and Brecht is both bemusing and impressive.

Pages 53-54, "In My Memories ...":
The poem commemorates Radnóti's third trip to Paris in the summer of 1939 (as made clear

by the date of the poem and by line 6 "It's been a year").

Line 17 "Gyula sat facing me, and Zsuzsanna": the Ortutays, who accompanied the Radnótis to Paris. For a photograph showing all four of them in the Paris studio apartment of their hosts, the Károly Koffán's, see Baróti, p. 143.

Pages 55-56, "Second Eclogue":
The presumable identity of the "Pilot" in this piece is a sobering example of the futility of an excessively biographical approach to the poems. Literally interpreted, the pilot would, of course, have to be an American or British flight officer, and while it may be true that some of them were "scared on those missions" (line 27), the real historical question might be how much most such men care about poetry. The "Poet" inside the poem posits an interlocutor who is a philistine, and who yet knows enough to inquire about the poet's work. A strange encounter of the imagination with reality, indeed.

Page 57, "Friday":
Line 2 "The sun was taking its nap"; literally rendered, the original reads: "The sun was not as yet shining." While my version of the line is motivated by rhyme, I discover that the rhyme-word *nap* is also an interlingual pun. It is English for "afternoon rest" but Hungarian for "sun." Unlike Brodsky's poetry, Radnóti's does not take to overt wordplay, despite an occasional example that does contribute to our sense of the poet's dry humor.

Line 16 "all three of them are lost": compare the images of friends lost in war as shaped in this poem with those in "Fifth Eclogue" and in "À la recherche ... ."

Page 58, "Third Eclogue":
Line 11 "I teach": as stated in the Introduction, Radnóti was not able to obtain a teaching appointment, although he was clearly qualified for one. The biographical correlate of these two words was very probably either private tutoring, or, as Ortutay informs us *(Kortárs* 3: 655; Baróti, p. 14), classes the poet was allowed to teach at his father-in-law's private school of stenography. The level of instruction is unknown in either instance, but at the stenography school it would in no case have gone beyond the rudiments of spelling and grammar.

Line 28 "Greek amphora": the sole reference to Greek art in Radnóti's poetry, possibly a semiconscious allusion to Keats's "Ode on a Grecian Urn." Radnóti translated Keats's poem "On Seeing the Elgin Marbles."

Page 59, "Similes":
Lines 20-21 "the deep-voiced, clear / vowel *ú*": pronounced as in English *cool,* only with a higher degree of tenseness. Radnóti's fascination with the poetic potential of sounds and words puts him in a class with a fine, language-conscious poet like May Swenson.

Page 60, "Spring Is in Flight":
The fact that this "Preface to the Eclogues" should come between the "Third" and "Fourth" may seem puzzling, but, that point aside, it is eminently useful to have a "Preface" from the poet's own hand.

The hemistichs that close each of the three stanzas of the poem are attested, as modifications of the hexameter line, in other poems as well; for example, in "Slips of Paper," a late cycle, five of the ten poetic vignettes are in hexameters concealed by division of the normal line into two lines of text each. Here is a translation of the first two lines of "Corpse": "My, how the dead man has grown, / his toe now reaches the bedpost." We may call this prosodic game an instance of dry humor in Radnóti.

Line 22 "Sleeper awake from your sleep!": it may not be excessive here to overhear the Lutheran chorale and the cantata by J. S. Bach.

Page 64, "Winter Sunshine":
Line 19 "treasury cap": an article of clothing issued by the government as a part of unemployment compensation benefits.

Page 68, "Columbus":
The pattern suggests a formally innovative sonnet, one that would not be unworthy of E. E. Cummings. Other – rare – instances of the sonnet in Radnóti's poetry are "Winter Sunday" (with an extra quatrain at the end) and "Oh, Old Prisons" (a Shakespearean example).

The opening line, with the quaintly spelled entry in the explorer's diary, suggests reading of a major biography. Other fine details (in lines 6, 8, 9, 12, and 13) appear to confirm this.

Pages 69-70, "The Terrible Angel":
Line 18 "You gave him birth and died of it!": although Radnóti rather frequently alludes to his childhood and to his personal background (cf. "While Writing" and "Fourth Eclogue"), this and some passages in "Twenty-Eight Years" are two rare examples of such open reference to the tragic circumstances of his mother's death (see also Baróti, pp. 40-41).

Page 73, "Fifth Eclogue":
Dedication: György Bálint (1906-1943), writer and critic, an outstanding representative of leftist feuilleton in Hungary between the two world wars, and a voluminous translator of English and American literature. He died in the field hospital at Starii [*sic;* Stare] Nikolskoe, Ukraine, on 21 January 1943 (after Kenyeres, 1:90).

Page 74, "I Cannot Know":
This is an example of Radnóti's most warmly patriotic poetry, and the mention of "the home of Mihály Vörösmarty" (line 12) is no accident.

Line 29 "We are guilty without a doubt": the utmost limit of reproach, in Radnóti's poetry, against his countrymen (cf. "Eighth Eclogue," lines 29-31).

Page 77, "May Picnic":
This genre picture of Hungarian teenagers should be particularly appealing to the American reader. The concluding five lines of the poem are all the more poignant when read against the fact that the poem was written almost two months after the German occupation of Hungary (19 March 1944) and but ten days before Radnóti's third and final callup for forced labor.

Page 78, "Dream Landscape":
Dedication: the German romantic poet Clemens Brentano (1778-1842), co-editor of *Des Knaben Wunderhorn,* was a master at precisely this brand of pure nature lyric. Nor would Radnóti's emotion, as expressed at the end, be alien to the romantic poet; only the closing couplet is peculiar to the modern poet's style. See also "Walk on, Condemned!", "Hymn to the Nile," and "Friday."

Pages 79-80, "Seventh Eclogue":
Line 14 "No diacritics": this is emphatically not true. Checking the appropriate place in the *Bor Notebook* facsimile, we find not only that every diacritical mark is scrupulously in place (in this poem as in every other), but also that the handwriting is clear, careful, indeed calli-

graphically beautiful. It is evident that the poet first thought out the poems by day and then wrote them down, at night, in final form. Only "Eighth Eclogue" occurs in two drafts in the *Notebook*.

Pages 81-82, "Letter to My Wife":
Line 40 "The light of *2 x 2*": the enlightened sobriety of the multiplication table, of mathematics and of philosophy, a source of comfort to a man in Radnóti's straits.

Pages 84-85, "À la recherche ...":
Title: the allusion to Proust's great novel, especially in the work of one whose training was in French literature, hardly needs comment.
Line 5 "auvergnat gris": in the original *"szürkebarát"* (literally, "Gray Monk"), a wine of the Tokaj region made to resemble auvergnat gris.
Line 10, place names: three major wars of the poet's lifetime.

Page 88, "Forced March":
Line 13 "tell me it's all still there": during summers the Radnótis spent their free time in an old vintner house in the Buda hills (on Istenhegy; address: Bp. XII, Diana-út 15/b.), where the novelist Mór Jókai also visited, according to tradition. There were the large summer house, and an enormous garden, with fruit trees. The place is celebrated in "Istenhegy Garden" (see Baróti, pp. 116-19), and in "Forced March." In winters the couple enjoyed skiing (cf. "Winter Sunday" and Ortutay, *Kortárs* 3:655; Baróti, p. 14; photos, ibid., pp. 120-21).
Line 19 "tonight's full moon": here a symbol of hope. Cf. the clouded moon in "Sky with Clouds" and the crescent moon of the poet's solitude in "Fourth Eclogue."

Pages 89-90, "Picture Postcards":
The four sections under this title (with four very different places and dates of composition) are written down in the *Bor Notebook* as four distinct poems. Number 1 occurs between "Eighth Eclogue" and "Forced March," and numbers 2, 3, and 4 follow in succession after the latter. Following the printing in the 1966 edition, the four "Postcards" are here presented as a single closing piece.
Title: in the original it is *"Razglednicák"*: Serbo-Croatian *razglednica* "picture postcard" supplied with the Hungarian nominative plural ending. Radnóti's probably limited knowledge of Serbo-Croatian may well have been acquired at "Lager Heidenau."
Number 2, lines 5-6: what the original tries to do with *o, p,* and *r* sounds in its attempt to convey the feeling of an image, I try to reproduce through use of *l, p,* and *s*. Elsewhere too the translator either has this kind of luck or tries to come by it without either forcing or distorting the meaning in the original.
Number 4, line 6 *"Der springt noch auf"*: some critics feel that Radnóti is here "covering" for his countrymen and that it was almost beyond a doubt Hungarian *nyilasok* ("Arrow Cross" troops, Hungary's infamous Nazi arm) rather than German SS men who executed Radnóti. From an objective standpoint this makes very little difference, of course. A potentially more fruitful view might stress, here as elsewhere, the poet's fascination with foreign languages.